One Farm Two Wars Three Generations

The Hege Family Story

Edith R

by Erica Hege Shirk

Erica Hege Shirk
Sept. 7, 1996

One Farm, Two Wars, Three Generations

Erica Hege Shirk
177 East Main Street
Leola, PA 17540

Cover Photograph
Schafbusch, the farm in Alsace
purchased by Peter Hege in 1912.

ISBN Number: 1-883294-36-3
Library of Congress Number: 96-75782

Printed by
Masthof Press
Route 1, Box 20
Morgantown, PA 19543

— Contents —

TO THE MEMORY
OF
OUR PARENTS

Philipp Hege
and
Emma Hirschler

— Preface —

"Write this as a reminder in a book." Exodus 17:14

In past years I have shared our family's war experiences in many churches, with senior citizens, and with women's groups. Invariably, someone said, "This story should be written in a book and published."

As a daughter in the family, my own life has been deeply affected. I realize such rich variety of experiences does not belong to the family alone. It should be passed on to posterity and beyond that to a larger circle of readers.

In fact, the story had been written by my oldest sister and printed in a booklet in French in 1986. In 1993 it was translated into German, at the request of German friends and relatives, by my sister-in-law, Ruth Hege Landes. My English version is based on the excellent work done by my sister Dora who worked with my father to compile the report.

The story is the dream of my father, Philipp Hege. It was his wish to preserve for his eighty-four grandchildren the history of the farm and the family's experiences of two World Wars. The availability of diaries, recently discovered letters, and a large selection of photos have been a valuable resource for me.

I wish to thank my family, especially my husband, who have encouraged and helped me not to give up until the work was done. It is my prayer that the book will bless many lives and bring glory to God.

- Erica Hege Shirk

HEGE FAMILY GENEALOGY

Hege Grandparents:

Peter Hege, 1872-1915
m. **Lina Hege**, 1874-1936
Children:
1. **Philipp Hege**, 1899-1979
   m. Emma Hirschler, 1897-1983
2. Frieda Hege, b. 1901
3. Lydia Hege, b. 1902
4. Otto Hege, b. 1903
5. Walter Hege, b. 1906
6. Hélène Hege, 1907-1927
7. Oscar Hege, b. 1910
8. Willy Hege, b. 1911
9. Hilde Hege, b. 1912

Hirschler Grandparents:

Johannes Hirschler, 1862-1910
m. **Marie Koller**, 1870-1958
Children:
1. Maria "Mimi" Hirschler, b. 1895
2. Heinrich Hirschler, b. 1896
3. **Emma Hirschler**, 1897-1983
   m. Philipp Hege, 1899-1979
4. Hélène Hirschler, b. 1898
5. Daniel Hirschler, b. 1899
6. Jakob Hirschler, b. 1900
7. Dina Hirschler, b. 1903
8. Elise Hirschler, b. 1907
9. Jean Hirschler, b. 1909

The Philipp and Emma (Hirschler) Hege Family

Philipp Hege, 1899-1979
m. **Emma Hirschler**, 1897-1983
Children:
1. Dora Hege, b. 1922
m. Jean Wenger
2. Ernest Hege, b. 1923
m. Madeleine Zehr
3. Irène Hege, 1924-1978
single
4. Alfred Hege, b. 1925
m. Ruth Landes
5. René Hege, b. 1927
m. Lydie Nussbaumer
6. Erica Hege, b. 1928
(Author of *One Farm, Two Wars, Three Generations*)
m. Frank Shirk
7. Eric Hege, 1928-1995
m. Anne Marie Eyer
8. Willy Hege, 1929-1995
m. Hedwig Landes
9. Fritz Hege, b. 1931
m. Ruth Nussbaumer
10. Uli Hege, 1932-1945
died young
11. Alice Hege, b. 1933
m. Charly Wenger
12. Oscar Hege, b. 1934
m. Jacqueline Jotter
13. Hans Hege, b. 1936
m. Edith Weiss
14. Louise Hege, b. 1937
m. André Nussbaumer
15. Martha Hege, 1939-1989
m. André Kauffmann
16. Théo Hege, b. 1939
m. Suzanne Reeb

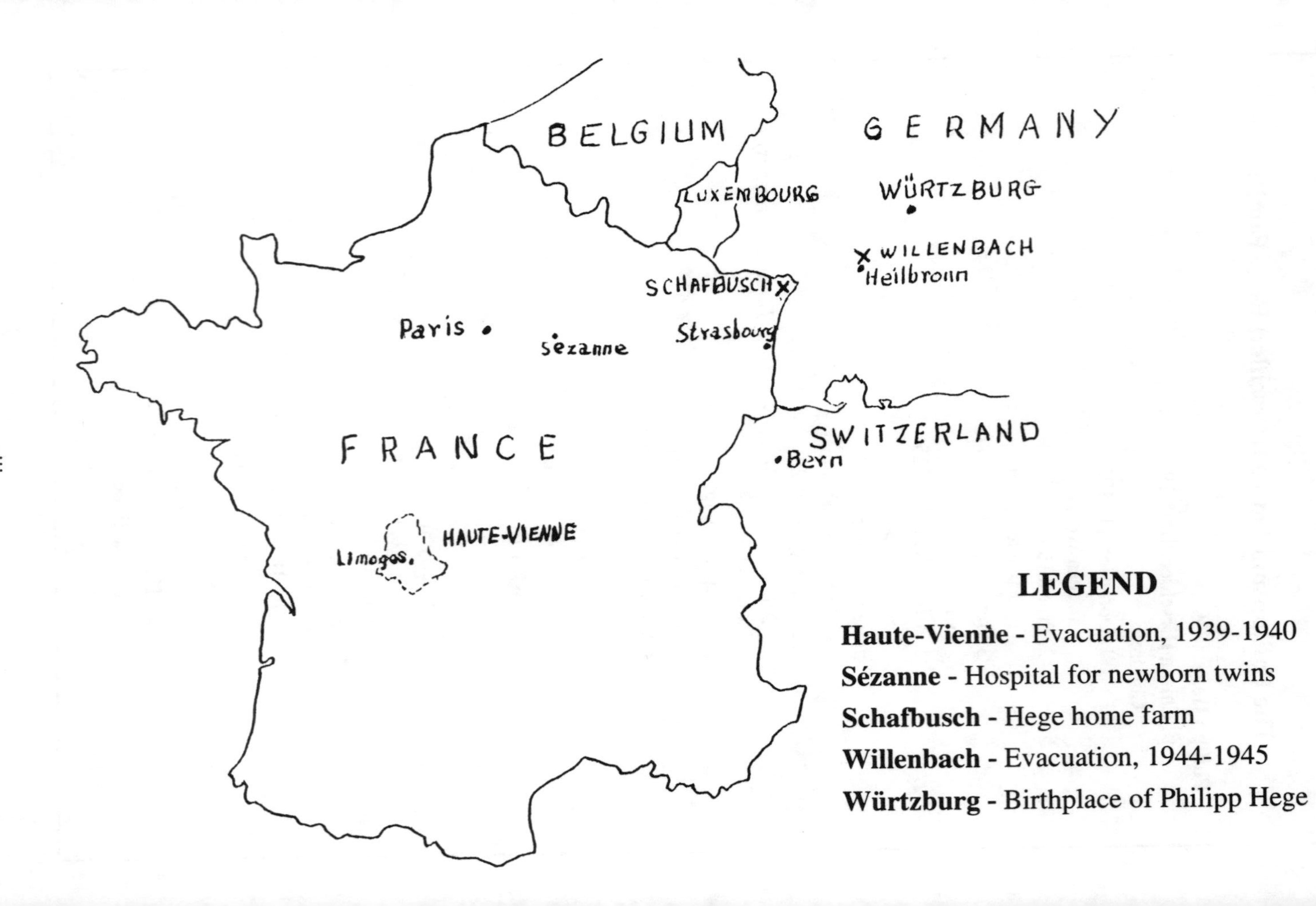
BELGIUM
GERMANY
LUXEMBOURG
WÜRTZBURG
WILLENBACH
Heilbronn
SCHAFBUSCH
Paris
Sézanne
Strasbourg
SWITZERLAND
Bern
FRANCE
HAUTE-VIENNE
LEGEND
Haute-Vienne - Evacuation, 1939-1940
Sézanne - Hospital for newborn twins
Schafbusch - Hege home farm
Willenbach - Evacuation, 1944-1945
Würtzburg - Birthplace of Philipp Hege

Your Grandfather Tells About His Life

Philipp Hege From 1899 to 1939

"Lord, you have been our dwelling place throughout all generations." Psalm 90:1

Introduction

I was born into a Mennonite family in Würtzburg, Germany, on Sunday, July 30, 1899. They gave me the name of my maternal grandfather: Philipp. I am the first child of my parents, Peter Hege, born on April 18, 1872, at the Spitalhof or Branchweilerhof near Neustadt at the Weinstrasse, and Lina Hege, born on November 2, 1874, at the Oberbiegelhof, near Babstadt-Baden (near Heilbronn). My father was the youngest son of Peter Hege and Babette (born Schmutz). My mother was the oldest daughter of Philipp Hege and Lene (born Landes). My paternal grandfather was a minister, my maternal grandfather an elder (bishop), each in their respective congregations. My father originated from the west side of the Rhine River. His family owned a farm around the end of the seventeenth or beginning of the eighteenth century. They were known to be hard-working farmers. Besides growing wheat, they also had vineyards and orchards. My mother's family also originated from the Palatinate from the same Hege line, but were not closely related. All my ancestors were Mennonites (Anabaptists) for generations and originated from Switzerland, driven out two centuries earlier because of their faith.

On the east side of the Rhine the Mennonites did not have the right to own property, but many were farmers on big estates belonging to the nobility. ("The fields are close by, the owner far away," was the saying.) Their financial situation was better than that of the small land owners on

Oberbiegelhof, the home farm of Lina Hege, mother of Philipp Hege, located near Heilbronn, Germany.

the west side of the Rhine. My maternal great-grandfather, Ulrich Hege, was the farmer at the big estate of Oberbiegelhof, an estate farmed by the same family for almost a century, until the estate, like many others, was bought by a sugar refinery. Because of the respect he had, and his good financial standing, this great-grandfather was able to find farms on similar estates for half a dozen of his sons.

From 1899 to 1912 at Schlüpferleinsmühle/Würtzburg (Germany)

After their marriage, my parents lived with my paternal grandparents at Spitalhof. At the age of more than seventy my grandfather was not yet ready to retire. In February 1899 my father began a search for a farm to rent and took over the large farm of the Schlüpferleinsmühle near Würtzburg. The estate of 125 hectares (300 acres) belonged to the hospital. A mill, which belonged to it, was rented out to a miller; but a distillery, used to transform potatoes from the farm into denatured alcohol, was part of the operation for a few years until it was sold by the owner. Since the barns on the property were really too small, the owner consented to finance the construction of an immense shed. This greatly facilitated the threshing and storing of grain.

Farming at the Schlüpferleinsmühle was done according to the methods of that time period. We had twenty to thirty dairy cows and were committed to deliver forty to fifty liters of milk to the hospital each day. The rest was sold to individuals in town. Each morning one of the men made the trip with his horse and wagon loaded with milk cans. When he

Peter Hege, Philipp's father, farmed this 300-acre farm, Schlüpferleinsmühle, near Würtzburg, Germany.

returned he had to give account to my father. At the beginning my father had a lot of problems finding stable men in charge of the milking. Either they walked off or they had to be sent away. Finally, he hired a married man, nicknamed "Swiss." This one stayed. Did he come from Switzerland? I don't know. In winter we fattened heifers with the waste products from the distillery called *Schlempe*.

For the field work there were four teams of horses, cared for by four hired men, each having the responsibility of one team. There was an additional horse for delivering milk, and also some oxen. In addition to the hired men, there were day laborers and seasonal workers. For the harvest, eight to ten men from a poor region were hired to cut the wheat with a scythe, tie it into sheaves, and stack them. The first few years a reaper binder was used, but later discontinued. The potatoes were also harvested by hand by local people. For each filled basket they received a metal token stamped with the initials of my father, P H. These were exchanged for pay at a later time. In later years the cultivation of potatoes was replaced with sugar beets. This work was done by a team of Polish seasonal workers who, from spring to fall, took care of hoeing, weeding, thinning of young plants and, finally, harvesting. All these operations were done by hand. A great number of workers were employed in this way. Even though wages were low, it took a lot of money on payday.

After the grain was cut a big threshing machine was brought in. It had a steam engine and a baler on which a man sat to tie knots on the bales. This was not yet done automatically. Most of the grain was sold right away and the rest was stored in the granary. I remember the year when my father sold 500 bags of barley for 10,000 German marks. Unfortunately, I cannot quote any other figures. For us, the children, the times of harvest and threshing were especially interesting. I remember being asked in 1911 to help load some barley. It was a prickly job and the barley made me itch all over. I resolved right then to never become a farmer. That same year I was to meet the threshing machine with a horse. For this I had to cross the town. The horse was scared and backed off each time a car passed. This happened at least a dozen times. Understandably, I was afraid, but did not let go of the horse. As soon as we reached the threshing machine we hitched it to it and started on the way back. To my astonishment the horse had lost all fear and did not shy even one time.

I went to school in Würtzburg. I had four years of primary school and two and a half years of secondary school (*Ober-Realschule*). Except for math, I was an average student. I had a hard time in French and made poor grades. I walked a distance of about three quarter hours to school. I took my noon meal with a Fellmann family where there were children my age and I had a lot of free time. I must confess that I succumbed to many temptations in the big city, knowing perfectly well that it was not good.

Today, I do not understand how I could have done certain things. We belonged to the Würtzburg congregation where my father served as minister. Almost every Sunday we walked two or three kilometers to church. My father had many contacts with Baptists, Methodists, and Darbists. Often I went with him on his visits. Later, he sent us, his children, to a Baptist Sunday School since the Mennonite churches had no Sunday School at that time. I learned many things there, for which I am still grateful today; nevertheless, I preferred going with my parents.

And then came a big change. By the end of 1911 our farming contract of twelve years expired. Our neighbor, Mr. Adami, who had a farm about the same size, had always been interested in the Schlüpferleinsmühle. At the time when the distillery was sold he had written an article in the newspaper in which he made it sound like the property had lost in value by giving up the license for the distillery (*Brennrecht*). On the other hand, he noted that my father was one of the best farmers who ever farmed that land. When the contract expired, Mr. Adami wrote to my father that he would like to rent the Schlüpferleinsmühle. Since my father always hoped to have his own farm, he decided to give up his lease in favor of his neighbor with the goal of buying another farm, knowing full well that his financial situation as owner would be less ideal. I remember the transactions that followed and the sum of money of 95,000 marks that the neighbor offered for the inventory and the livestock. My father had asked for 100,000; finally they agreed on 97,000 marks.

At Schafbusch near Wissembourg (Alsace)
Beginning April 15, 1912

So now we had to leave the Schlüpferleinsmühle. My father began the search for a farm. He received several offers, including some near Würtzburg. I do not know how he discovered the Schafbusch. It seems that he already knew of it by name. The property of Schafbusch is located three kilometers east of Wissembourg, on the south side of Geisberg, bordering the hamlet by the same name where there was (and still is today) a small Mennonite congregation. I think that this fact influenced my father's decision.

Some History

Mennonites have farmed Schafbusch since the beginning of the eighteenth century—several documents confirm this—first, a Schowalder family, spelled with a "d," followed by Hirschler families until 1906. The property was always rented to two farmers. After the French Revolution in 1789, the farmers from the Geisberg were able to buy their fields, which were much smaller; but, for the farmers of Schafbusch the sum to pay was much too high. It was a family from Wissembourg who bought it and sold it again in 1906 to a high official of the railroad from Karlsruhe, named Reichert, who did the farming himself. Until about 1840 Schafbusch was the meeting place for the Mennonites. Then during the period when there were no Mennonite farmers anymore, a meeting room was fixed up at Geisberg in the former pigeon tower.

The battle of Geisberg on August 4, 1870, deeply marked the inhabitants of Geisberg and Schafbusch. This is what Aunt Babette Hirschler, a

Schafbusch, the farm in Alsace purchased by Peter Hege in 1912.

An artist's drawing of the visit of Germany's Crown Prince Friedr. Wilhelm in the living room at Schafbusch. He came to pay tribute to the slain French General Abel Douay in the War of 1870.

young girl living at Schafbusch at the time, told your grandmother more than once:

On the evening before August 4, the owner, Herr Volpert, who had reserved two rooms on the first floor for his parties, had organized a drinking party for several French army officers. According to some sources, Abel Douay was among them. They stayed up till late that night. At dawn they were awakened by the sound of nearby gunfire from the Palatinate border. Panicking, they hid at first under their beds before getting a hold of themselves and deciding to join their units stationed in Wissembourg.

The battle of Geisberg lasted only two hours, from about 9:00 to 11:00 in the forenoon. Schafbusch was transformed into a military field hospital. A huge white flag with a red cross waved on the roof and many wounded soldiers were brought into the cellar. In the beginning of the morning General Abel Douay was carried in, mortally wounded. They laid him on one of our mattresses in the living room, the room to the left coming into the house. Since then this room was renamed "Abel Douay room." History reports that he was dying but in reality he was already dead when he arrived.

There was much coming and going by French and German soldiers. Around four in the afternoon we had the impression that an important event was happening. The soldiers stood at attention and a group of high officers appeared. With them was Crown Prince Friedrich Wilhelm, commander of the Prussian troops, who came to pay respect to the mortal remains of his adversary. His personal physician was with him. The French troops had retreated to Woerth. The painter, Anton v. Werner, has depicted this scene in one of his paintings.

After these officers left, the German soldiers began to plunder the farm and took along anything that could be eaten, especially a very large bowl of raspberry dessert which had been prepared for the wedding reception of Aunt Babette. The families from Geisberg had also been robbed of their most basic necessities. The German Mennonites organized relief from Althof (today Bonartshauserhof) near Bretten. They came with one or two horse-drawn wagons loaded with food.

In 1912 my father discussed his project with his brother, Uncle Jacob from Kohlhof, who informed him that Schafbusch was not worth making the trip. However, Father decided to go and he asked his brothers-in-law, Uncle Philipp Hege from Mückenhäuserhof (Worms), and Uncle Heinrich Funck from Althof to accompany him. It was easy to see that the farm was poorly managed. The present owner was clearly not a farmer. Nevertheless, Father decided to buy the property and signed the contract in March 1912. We could take possession on the following April 15. The property included forty-five hectares of land in one plot and worth 130,000 marks. Later, we rented another twenty hectares. Since the property was burdened with a mortgage of 70,000 marks, Father was able to pay cash and had a certain sum of money left over for remodeling and new equipment.

Now it was time to leave Würtzburg. With my parents we made many good-bye visits in the congregation; they were all sorry to see us go. From all sides there was disapproval for my father's decision to leave. The following years, which would be so heavy with trials, were going to justify these fears. The day of our departure was approaching. The youngest brothers and sisters had already been taken to Mückenhäuserhof; later the parents followed with the older ones. When my father took the train to Wissembourg I naturally wanted to come along. Getting there, Father had some errands to do in town. I started out alone, on foot of course, in the direction of Schafbusch. There I was greeted by one of our former hired men who had been sent ahead of us. Uncle Jacob from Kohlhof was there and soon my father also arrived.

My first impressions of the house and the farm buildings were very disappointing. There was no electricity or running water. (Electricity was not installed until 1954.) There were many other things I didn't like. On the other hand, there was a telephone: number 17. During the noon meal Uncle Jacob was in conversation with the mother-in-law of the previous owner who was a widower. She complained that the owner would like to retire to the little house across the road, but his son conducted himself so awkwardly and would never succeed in getting married. (Later, this son married my mother's sister.) I remember the fear that got hold of me thinking about my future marriage.

On our return trip to Mückenhäuserhof I got off the train in Neustadt to visit my grandfather. Finally, on April 15, 1912, my parents, with some of the children, boarded the train with three containers of our possessions and we moved to Schafbusch. At first it was not very inviting. All the rooms were being freshly painted. Everything was cold and unfriendly, and we didn't feel at home. The hired man responsible for millking, who had promised to stay, disappeared the same evening, leaving us with twenty cows to milk. However, the next day, and thanks to the telephone, the employment agency in Strasbourg sent us a capable man who stayed for some time.

Easter vacation came to an end and it was time to start school in Wissembourg. At the high school, Latin was a required subject and I was to make up the three years in three six-week sessions through private lessons. I was soon very discouraged. Besides, I had great difficulties to adjust in other areas also. Thus, I dropped out of high school before the beginning of summer vacation. In the fall I entered secondary school (*Mittelschule*) where French was taught but not Latin. I liked it there much better. I was able to keep up, and even got good grades in French. Father would have liked for me to continue until I was sixteen and obtain the one-year certificate, *Einjährige Zeugnis.* Military service was reduced from two years to one for the owner of this certificate. But, it turned out that at Wissembourg this certificate was not issued. So I could not see any use to continue my studies.

"Well," said my father, "since this is so you will be a farmer." So, beginning the spring of 1913, I became an apprentice farmer in the family business. Since I had started school in the fall of 1905 and had stopped in the spring of 1913, my schooling lasted only seven and a half years instead of eight. This explains why there are many things that I don't know! My father gave me a variety of things to do. I asked many questions and in this way I learned a lot. I also took courses in a winter school during the winter of 1913-1914.

The year 1912 was a difficult year. It rained often and it wasn't until mid-September that a poor grain harvest could be gathered in. In 1913 and 1914 Father hired seven Polish workers who were responsible for the cultivation of ten hectares of sugar beets. The fields were very weedy, especially couch-grass, thistles, and yellow and white mustard. We had to first pull out the weeds by hand before being able to thin out the plants. While working on this job the thought came to me: one should be able to use poison to control these weeds!

Some fields were too wet and had to be drained. Father began this immense project the very first winter. For this he dug parallel trenches at twelve-meter intervals and at 1.20-meter depth. He put in drainage tiles of 30 centimeters in length and 5 to 10 centimeters in diameter. All this work was done by hand during the slow season by a team of ten to twelve day workers from the village of Riedseltz. The work was finally finished in 1923.

We fattened a few pigs for our own use. Little by little we eliminated the beef cattle, keeping only two or three dairy cows. Father hoped to farm the land without raising cattle. He was influenced by his farmer relatives, especially his brother-in-law, Philipp Hege from Mückenhäuserhof, who had good results. He was also impressed by the conclusions of a research paper done by the cousin of my mother. I still have in my possession this study under the title: "Nutzviehschwache Wirtschaft (The Weakness of Cattle Raising) of Ulrich Hege of Häusern near München." The author is Dr. Friedrich Wagner and publisher, Eugen Ulmer, Stuttgart, 1912. At that time Germany had to import grain but was well supplied with dairy products.

At the same time Father undertook the remodeling of the buildings. First the house, which had been built as a double house. The thick middle wall was taken out to create a large hallway. A bathroom and running water were installed. A holding tank in the attic was filled each day with a hand pump and later was operated with a gasoline motor. To finance all these improvements, Father took out a loan on the house from a well-known Jewish horse dealer. Over the years all the hard work and improvements bore fruit and became the subject of admiration and astonishment in the area.

A little story which happened around this time is told by my brother Oscar: "In 1914 an airplane made an emergency landing in our sugar beet field. What excitement! People came in large numbers to examine it. It stayed well guarded for one or two days. I remember a policeman wanted to chase me away but with my father at my side I was allowed to stay." The same thing happened again in the thirties: a German plane landed in our field; the pilot thought he was on German territory. He was arrested and his plane stored in one of our barns. It was guarded for several months by the French army. In later years gliders made emergency landings on our fields.

During the First World War, 1914-1918

War broke out in August 1914. In the Alsace, a border area, stricter measures were used for the general mobilization. In the first days men from 39 to 45, like my father, were called for service. All the steps taken to keep him home and all the protests were of no use. He had to leave his family of nine minor children and the big farm behind. In the fall of 1914 Father came home twice for a short leave. The second time he arrived at seven in the evening during the last hours of wheat threshing. When he left again it was the last we were to see him. The first months Father was stationed in

Schirmeck, but in February he was sent to Poland. Actually, all the Alsatian soldiers were sent east. Their sympathy for France was not to be trusted. Even though these reservists were not to fight in the front lines, my father's regiment was quickly mixed up in a battle during which he was wounded and taken prisoner. He sent us mail from Warsaw, later from Moscow, and then no more. It was not until 1924 that we heard for certain that he had died of typhoid fever at Taschkent on June 27 or 28, 1915.

So, at age fifteen, I had to take the place of my father. On that first morning my mother woke me at five with the words: "Get up and give the men their assignments. They are waiting outside and don't know what to do." Since it had rained that night it was clear that we could not continue the harvest. I made a tour of the farm and found some work for each of the men. Four of our six horses had been requisitioned and one of the hired man was called up for the army. To bring in the harvest I had two hired men, three Poles, four women and young girls. I also had two horses that had been rejected by the army and two cows. The men cut the grain with long scythes, the women followed along and tied the sheaves with strands of straw.

On the first days of harvest, it was the custom for the reapers to tie a ribbon on my arm, and when the harvest was all brought in they offered me a wreath of wheat. In return I gave them a generous tip. For the threshing a big threshing machine, powered by a steam engine, was rented at seven or eight marks per hour. In addition we housed and fed the owner of the machine and his two helpers. Some refugees from the valley of Munster came and were a valuable help.

In 1915, we rented a large threshing machine powered by a steam engine. Standing from right to left is Oscar, Frieda, Hilde, Helene, Willy, Lydia, Walter, Otto, the machine owner, and his employees.

After the wheat harvest was finished it was time to bring in the potatoes. It was a rather meager harvest. Then we harvested ten hectares of sugar beets. This last job occupied us until the end of the year. We pulled out the beets, one by one, by hand, laid them in rows, cut off the leaves with a sickle, put them on piles, and covered them with the greens. Since the beets could not be delivered right away, we temporarily filled wagons and dumped them in the farmyard. All these jobs were done by hand, of course. Finally, in December we were able to start delivering the sugar beets. By Christmas we had loaded thirty-two box cars at the train station in Wissembourg at the rate of two cars a day, moving some 500 tons, all by hand.

After September we were able to get two additional horses and several oxen. By October we had seeded some of the wheat fields and, as time permitted, plowed others. The following spring the army loaned us a third horse and we could get a pair of oxen from the Mückenhäuserhof. This way we were able to seed the rest of the fields. But the weeds got the upper hand and grew lustily until harvest. That summer it rained less and we planted fewer sugar beets. I was a little more experienced and everything went better. Now, I thought I knew it all; but not for long!

The year 1916 was very difficult. I learned a lot. I realized more than anything that I was still very ignorant and incapable. It rained much. Not having a cleaning machine to sort out the weeds from the grain, we had seeded thirteen hectares of rye mixed with vetch. By mid-May the rye and the vetch started to bloom. The vetch spread over everything so that we could no longer walk through the fields. Besides, it rained again and again. The vetch grew and got ahead of the rye; it was one big field of blue flowers. It was hard work at harvest time. The other grain could be stored in the barn, but we had to pile the rye, loose, outside in the courtyard. The threshing took extra time, the results were poor, and the selling price low since the rye was damp and mixed with innumerable black vetch seeds. Finally, that year came to an end also. At that time I kept a journal and made a note that the horses either had to work too hard, or were resting longer than necessary. So, some of the work could not get done on time.

The year 1917 was an easier year. By the end of the year a German officer, wounded from the war, from the recovery company, rented a part of our land—eighteen hectares at 300 marks per hectare. From that time on, it was easier to manage the rest of the farm. I was even tempted to sell off some land to pay the debts which had accumulated. Fortunately, this never happened.

Between the Two Wars, 1918-1939

In November 1918 the armistice was signed. At the same time the "Spanish flu" was going around. There were many victims in the area, but our family was spared.

In 1919 the Alsace was reunited with France. The residents were classified in four categories, each receiving different identity cards according to origin:

Class A: the "pure," born in Alsace by an Alsacien father (for example: my future wife).
Class B: the "mixed blood" (like my future mother-in-law; German from the Palatinate but married to an Alsacien).
Class C: the neutrals (for example, the Swiss).
Class D: the "foreign enemies," that is, the Germans and their relatives, like our family.

At first that identity card did not allow us to exchange marks into francs. This was permitted later, but at a less advantageous rate. What was even more serious was that we were supposed to leave the country with only 30 kgs of luggage per person. At the beginning of the war we had lost our father because the German government had treated him like an Alsacien citizen; now we were going to lose our farm and home after the war because the French government treated us like Germans. The farm was confiscated. I was asked to keep accurate records while waiting for the farm to be sold at auction, with the proceeds going to the French government. After that, we were to leave the country.

Life continued as usual; the seasonal work followed the normal rhythm, as if nothing had happened. The possibility of an expulsion didn't bother us very much, which still surprises me today. The representative of the sugar refinery had delayed the payment of the last delivery of beets until a more favorable exchange rate. This money got us through until the next harvest. We had no fertilizer but, thanks to favorable weather, the harvest was fairly good. In 1920 the sale of our farm by auction was advertised. Our Jewish grain buyer, Mr. Levy, put us in touch with the rabbi from Wissembourg who intervened in our favor and obtained a residence permit for us. (In the Alsace, the Jews and the Anabaptists felt a certain kinship of trial since they both lived on the margin of society and suffered the same misunderstanding by the population.) The confiscation was lifted and we could stay. In this way our Heavenly Father delivered and protected us in His marvelous way during this critical period. In 1928 my mother was naturalized with all her children except Otto.

Let us return now to the threshing. Until 1918 a threshing machine was rented from the village of Schaidt. During the winter of 1919 we were able to use the machine from Deutschhof. The following year I bought a used machine operated by a gasoline motor. The harvest had been good

This Cormick 8/16 four-cycle tractor was purchased in 1923. It had iron wheels and no lights.

but there were many problems, annoyances, and losses of time until the engine ran smoothly. We threshed in the summer, in the fall, and into the winter. It was enough to despair!

1921 was a dry year and all the grain ripened at the same time. To make faster progress we used the binder that my father had bought in 1913. Our Polish harvesters were compensated for lost wages. Oscar hasn't forgotten those days. He tells this story: "My brother Willy and I took turns staying home from school; it was our job to take away the sheaves at the end of the field and to make sure there was room for the binder. We had to do it because our big brothers were too lazy to get off the machine and do the work themselves."

Now we could bring in the harvest from the field and unload directly into the threshing machine. Oscar has vivid memories of this: "The two little brothers, Willy and Oscar, had to take away the bales and swallow tons of dust doing it. As a reward we received an erector set for Christmas. Frieda, our oldest sister, however, thought we didn't deserve such a present!"

After this, my work became easier, even when it rained a lot, as was the case the following year. I had learned my lessons from the difficult experiences and improved my methods and techniques constantly. I kept a record of my observations and made graphs to divide the workload. I regularly read and studied German farm magazines.

In 1922 I ordered the first tractor, a Fordson, but it could not be delivered. They returned the down payment in installments. The following year, however, I was able to buy a Cormick 8/16 with four cylinders. It had iron wheels and no lights. This was the beginning of a new era for Schafbusch; the only tractor in all the country. It was used to plow, pull the

The horses were still needed to pull wagons and do other jobs.

reaper-binder, and activate the threshing machine. This brought considerable improvements. We still used four horses for pulling the wagons on the road and to do other jobs.

Two years later, we began raising peas for the Auer cannery in Wissembourg. They were grown on the two-hectare *Buckenmeir* field. It was easy to find people for pea picking in the surrounding villages. They came from Schleithal, Seebach, Riedseltz, Kapsweiher, and especially from Weiler.

People for pea picking came from the surrounding villages.

Women from the village of Schleithal came to pick peas in their traditional dress.

The following year, already, we planted more peas. Some years we planted as much as twelve hectares. Pickers were informed through announcements in the newspaper and through the town crier in the village square. There were as many as 200 persons a day, men and women, dressed in their village costumes. Sometimes six to eight gypsy families came, univited, in their trailers. They camped near the farm and made their raids in the neighborhoods. Finally, because the people in the area complained, they had to be sent away. My brother, Oscar, has this memory of the first pea pickers: "I was then only fourteen years old and it was my job to assign the pickers their places, which made me feel very uncomfortable." Later, and until 1939, the peas were delivered to the Ungemach cannery in Strasbourg. We also produced string beans for them, and also for the Auer cannery in Wissembourg.

After the war a specialized threshing machine replaced the pickers. It was stationed either at our farm or in Oberseebach. The entire plants were mowed and piled on wagons and transported to the threshing machine. In 1929 I bought a second improved Cormick tractor, still with iron wheels; also, a new binder, and the following year a threshing machine with baler. We organized the work so that we could unload the harvest directly from the field into the threshing machine. We gradually improved this system. The children pushed the bales of straw on rails from one section to the next to fill up the barn.

The three Polish families who lived and worked on the farm left one after another, finding better paying jobs in town. The men had helped with the farm work, and the women with the garden, laundry, and cleaning. In the meantime my brothers Otto, Walter, Oscar, and Willy helped in the farm operation, at least some of the time. To gain practical experience each worked

Around 1939, we produced seed potatoes for the FaberHouse Seed Company in Metz.

for a time on other Mennonite farms; at Muntzenheim, at Schoppenwihr, at Niederhof, and at Mückenhäuserhof. We employed different young men from Alsace and the Palatinate over the years. Ten or fifteen day workers came from Riedseltz for seasonal work.

In 1937, two young men and two young girls came from Poland; all four were very capable and good workers. Cash was scarce during those years and was used almost entirely for the salaries of the employees. My brothers received only a modest allowance. We never bought vegetables, fruit, or bread, and only seldom meat, except some beef for Sunday dinner and some lunch meat during the summer. We never asked for credit at the bank. Through improvements and better organization we increased production. There was a growing demand for potatoes which sold not only for human consumption but also for seed and animal feed. At the beginning of the war, in 1939, when we left for the Haute Vienne, we had twelve hectares of the precious tubers in the ground. The wheat was sold as certified seed since 1923. This assured a higher sale price. Around 1939, we produced beets, string beans, and potatoes for the Faber House seed company in Metz. Almost every year we planted experimental plots of wheat and potatoes. It was a challenging experience. At first I did this for my own experimentation, but later, in cooperation with the Institute of National Agronomic Research in Colmar, with grain only.

In the past, until the appearance of the potato beetle, very little spraying was done on fruit trees and none in the fields. I bought the first sprayer on wheels in 1938, the second of its kind sold in France. It was pulled by a horse and activated by a gasoline engine. After World War II it was necessary to get a larger sprayer for a tractor because of an increasing need to treat on a larger scale; potatoes were treated for the beetle and diseases, the grain for weeds and diseases. In 1939 the first potato beetles appeared, but the damage of this insect was never as considerable as it was feared. Because of all these efforts, the yields increased and the income accordingly. We could realize some new construction and purchase other machines which made the work easier. Our farm was considered a model enterprise and was visited by numerous groups and associations. In 1932, the government awarded us the "Outstanding French Farmer" title. Two years later, I was named *Chevalier de Mérite Agricole* (Knight of Agricultural Merit) and on March 17, 1951, Officer of the same designation, both without a special ceremony.

My mother and her children, from the right (seated): Hilde, Mother, Hélène, and Oscar (standing). Back row (from the right): Willy, Walter, Lydia, Philipp, Frieda, and Otto.

My Mother, Brothers, and Sisters

From the day my father was called into the army, I began to manage the farm. I was age fifteen. Mother seldom intervened in the organization of the work. In general, the work-

My father, Peter Hege. In 1914, he was drafted into the German army and died of typhoid fever in Russia the next year.

ers listened to me; I think they supposed I was carrying out my mother's orders. On the other hand, we always discussed the money matters together. Generally Mother approved my projects.

Mother's brother from Mückenhäuserhof came from time to time to give advice and financial support. The uncertainty about her husband caused my mother much suffering, affecting her health. Fortunately, my sisters, Frieda and Lydia, helped with the household work. In 1934 she retired and lived with my youngest sister, Hilde, and my unmarried brothers, Walter, Oscar, and Willy. Frieda, Lydia, and Otto married during her lifetime.

Mother experienced the grief of losing two sons-in-law, seeing her two daughters become widows with five and four small children. In 1927, her daughter, Hélène, died accidentally at the age of twenty. Hélène had gone to Deutschhof, Germany, to help her sister Frieda with the laundry. When her clothes caught on fire she panicked and ran outside, which revived the flames all the more. The Red Cross ambulance was not authorized to enter France, so she had to be picked up at the border by a taxi. There was no treatment for serious burns available at that time. The doctor prescribed strong coffee and warm baths twice a day to relieve the suffering. Three days later Hélène died at Schafbusch.

When I told my mother about my plans to get married she said God had already prepared her to give her consent. We were married in 1921, but mother did not divide the inheritance until 1936. At that time I took over the farm. My mother was quite ill with a heart condition and died a few

My mother enjoyed her grandchildren.

months later. Some brothers and sisters had received sums of money earlier. For my work of twenty-two years a specified salary was estimated, and also an amount for the work of my brothers and sisters. There remained some debts. Finally, I proposed an amount which I thought was fair for taking over the farm. My mother, brothers, and sisters approved it; a notary drew up the legal papers. It was several years after World War II that I was able to make the last payments to my brothers and sisters.

Frieda and her husband moved to Deutschhof; Lydia to Geisberg, where she remained after being widowed. Otto rented a small farm at Petit-Landau (Haut-Rhin) in 1932. This proved to be a failure. The harvests were poor so that he gave up and came back to Schafbusch with his family in 1938. He stood by me in my work until 1952 and I appreciated his help very much. Walter rented the small farm of the Roth family of Geisberg which had been sold to M. Vincent from Haguenau. Willy operated the farm of his parents-in-law. Oscar became the manager of the Schoppenwihr estate north of Colmar. Hilde spent several years with a Fellmann family before training as a nurse. She moved to Thomashof, a Mennonite center near Karlsruhe, to serve as a deaconess. Out of there she was available to help in Mennonite families.

Life in the Geisberg Mennonite Congregation

My wife's great uncle, cousin Hannes, was minister and elder of the Geisberg Mennonite congregation since 1907. My wife, however, does not remember ever hearing him preach. Her father was the deacon. My father was a minister from 1912 to 1914.

At Deutschhof the only minister was cousin Daniel Schmitt, father of Friedrich and Otto Schmitt, but only until 1915. For six years the congregations of Geisberg, Haftelhof, and Deutschhof were without a minister. We rotated services at Deutschhof, Haftelhof, and Geisberg, bringing in ministers from the outside. Generally, we went on foot to Haftelhof and sometimes even to Deutschhof, a walk of two hours. I felt sorry for the horse that had worked hard all week.

Instruction for baptism was done by the visiting ministers. A two-week concentrated course was held by our itinerant evangelist, Gysbert van der Smissen. I knew by memory all the questions and answers of the instruction manual. I was baptized in 1916, along with my sisters Frieda and Lydia, as well as several other young people from the congregation. My baptism made a deep impression on me and I resolved to be a more committed Christian. Nevertheless, when life was easy I neglected Bible reading and prayer, only to come back to it with more zeal during hard times. I am grateful to my Lord who brought me back to Himself each time I had gone astray.

After 1921, four ministers were ordained. Friedrich Schmitt from Niederroedern; my brother-in-law, Otto Schmitt; his brother Friedrich; and

Rudolph Hege. The last three lived at Deutschhof. I have served as minister since 1928. I still remember how deeply I was affected when I learned that a minister was to be chosen at Geisberg. I understood right away that I would be the one. It was not easy for me to speak, and I was not gifted at preaching. But, in obedience and out of love for my Lord and the congregation, I accepted this responsibility. The first three years I wrote down the whole sermon, word for word. Later I learned to speak using only a few notes. It was not always easy to find a text and the necessary comments. I was never quite satisfied with my preaching; how many times I wished someone would come and take this responsibility from me.

Yet, each time when it was my turn I took up the task with the desire to do a better job. Soon I was also given the responsibility for baptismal instruction. God gave the needed grace. I know of many mistakes, but God straightened out much that was crooked. In looking back over almost fifty years of ministry, I recognize that I was abundantly rewarded. How many times I experienced answers to my prayers for the congregation. I was forced to study the Word and to pray. If I had not accepted this responsibility, my life would have taken a different course. I am grateful to our congregations for their patience with me.

My brother Willy, Fritz Hirschler, and August Schowalter were ordained as ministers in 1937; the first two at Geisberg, the latter at Deutschhof. In 1943, during the war, Rudolf Hege, August Schowalter, and I were ordained as elders. Aunt Madeleine Hirschler taught the children in Sunday School, but not very regularly because of her many visits to Pfastatt. In 1930 she asked my wife to replace her. She, however, convinced my brother Willy to teach in her stead. After that, Fritz Hirschler became the Sunday School uncle. In those days Sunday School took place on Sunday afternoon.

Our Family Life

There is a song, "When Grandfather married Grandmother...." That was in 1921. There is obviously more to this but, to the great disappointment of my children, grandchildren, and great-grandchildren, this will remain my secret. What I can say today, in 1976, five years after our golden wedding anniversary is, that I am still grateful to have taken this step in the will of God who has shown us the way. In a remarkable way I still remember two or three dreams which showed me the will of God in this most important decision. He has led everything wonderfully and I will always be grateful to my companion for having said "yes" many years ago.

My wife, Emma Hirschler, was born at Geisberg (Alsace) on August 25, 1897, the third of nine children. On April 14, 1921, there was a big

The double wedding at Chateau Geisberg.
The bridal couple on the right is Emma and Philipp Hege.

Wedding photo of Philipp Hege and Emma Hirschler on April 14, 1921.

celebration at the Chateau Geisberg—a double wedding. The sisters Emma and Mimi Hirschler were married to Philipp Hege and Daniel Ehrismann, respectively.

Grandmother writes:

"The date for the ceremony was set for April 14, 1921. It was the first wedding after the war. All the people of Geisberg participated in the festivities, held in the spacious rooms of the Chateau. Some residents from Deutschhof 'risked' crossing the border. It was a happy celebration which many still remember. My sister married Daniel Ehrismann and remained at Geisberg."

Grandather continues:

Until 1934 we kept house with my mother and my unmarried brothers and sisters. Over the years we had sixteen children.

We welcomed each child with joy. God was gracious and my wife, your grandmother, remained in good health. Usually she had the necessary household help. She had hired girls, someone for sewing and mending, and extra help as needed. The children were equally in good health and our Lord preserved them from serious illnesses and accidents. We had no health insurance; the family doctor sent his fee at the end of the year. I remember one year there was no bill because we didn't need his services. Before 1939 we received a family allocation, but I can no longer give specific details.

The family of Philipp and Emma Hege in 1944 with sixteen children. "We welcomed each child with joy."

We always had hail and fire insurance. The car was insured, also. It was not until after the war that I took out private health insurance.

We bought our first car in 1928, a Renault-Torpedo with seven seats. It was used sparingly. My wife continued to walk to town; later she used the bus, Strasbourg-Wissembourg, which passed in front of our house. The schoolchildren walked to Wissembourg in all kinds of weather. The roads were in bad condition. The one in front of our house was not paved until 1929. We seldom traveled. To visit our relatives in Germany at Althof or at Mückenhäuserhof we had to have a passport and visa.

"Our first car was a Renault-Torpedo bought in 1928. It had seven seats."

The absence of electricity limited our possibilities for equipment. Bread was kneaded by hand, the laundry was done without a washing machine. A whole series of oil lamps and lanterns had to be shined and filled twice a week. In order to feed the fifteen to twenty-three family members and employees who lived on the farm, we had to grow lots of vegetables and small fruit. For winter we canned and preserved fruit and meat in glass jars, tin cans, and wooden barrels. We made jam and we dried apples, mirabelles, and plums in the bake oven; we made sauerkraut. We butchered up to six hogs a year, and then salted and smoked the meat. Each day had a full measure of labor and duties. In spite of all the hard work, it was a happy time.

The only house at Geisberg that survived World War II. It was here that Emma (Hirschler) Hege was born.

Childhood and Youth Memories of Your Grandmother

Emma (Hirschler) Hege From 1897-1939

(Compiled from notes found after her death)

You are all acquainted with the only house of earlier days, which survived the war, at the entrance of Geisberg, called "am Tor" (at the gate). The family of my parents, Jean and Marie Hirschler, lived in this house at the end of the last century. To differentiate them from the other four Hirschler families living at Geisberg, they were called the "Eliasse," after the name of my grandfather. It is here that I was born on August 25, 1897. I was the third of nine children and they named me Emma.

The paternal grandparents lived with us, as well as two unmarried sisters of my father: "Sanchedande" (Aunt Suzanne) and "Madleedande"

Jean/John Hirschler, father of Emma Hege, died of pneumonia in 1910 at age forty-six.

(Aunt Madeleine). Aunt Suzanne married and became the mother of Max, Elizabeth, and Hans Schowalter; Aunt Madeleine remained single. Grandmother took care of the cooking; Aunt Suzanne helped everywhere. Aunt Madeleine made our clothes. She was a capable, energetic woman who felt called to take over our training. Some of us didn't very well accept the spankings she administered.

The two sisters enjoyed handcrafts, knitting, crocheting, embroidering, tatting, lace making, and also woodburning. At an early age they taught these to my sister and me, and passed along their enjoyment. In the evening and on Sunday there was singing with the zither and mandolin. We learned new hymns and folk songs, constantly enriching our repertoire.

My mother worked in the barn and in the fields; in winter she helped with the threshing. Very rarely could she be found sitting by the fire, knitting. When she did, she would gather us around and tell us stories in such a vivid and captivating way that just to think of it, even now, my heart is warmed. She had a very beautiful voice and sang almost all the time while working, either humming or singing out loud. She knew many hymns from the song book, *Frohe Botschaft*, as well as folk songs she had learned in her parental home at Stockborn (Palatinate) where singing was an individual and family passion. I remember accompanying my mother when she visited her parents and spending unforgettable hours singing with my cousins.

My father was a hard worker, an alert farmer and animal breeder, a lover of bees, and a fruit grower. He was attentive to the needs of his family

The family of Jean and Marie Hirschler, right to left: Mimi, Jean, Maria (mother), and Elise. Behind Elise is Emma, Jacob, Dina, Heinrich, and Daniel. In the window is Elias (grandfather).

and loved his children. On summer evenings, at the end of a hard day, he rested, sitting on the bench in front of the house with all of us gathered around him. We discussed the events of the day and sang until the stars shone in the sky, and then it was time to go to sleep.

Early in the morning both parents went to the barn. Mother milked the cows, then came in to waken the schoolchildren and prepare breakfast, which consisted of a soup made with browned flour (the flour was roasted in advance). The children didn't like it very much, but that did not make any difference! At seven o'clock we left for school. In all kinds of weather we walked to Wissembourg, a good three kilometers. In winter it was still dark. Mother adjusted the scarves around our heads and, wrapped up and closely bunched together, we headed into the cold and the wind. In spring it was more pleasant when the sun shone and Father allowed us to take the shortcut through the meadow where the larks trilled in the sky and the rabbits hopped across the fields. The boys went to the Protestant boys' school in the rue de l'Ecole and the girls went to the Protestant girls' school in the rue de 'Etoile.

The day after the wedding, Philipp came to pick up Emma in a horse-drawn carriage similar to this one.

We were usually the first ones there. During the noon hour we stayed in our classroom to eat our lunch. Mother had prepared a pail with milk coffee, which we heated on the school's coal stove, and an enormous sandwich with butter and honey. Sometimes there were variations: liver sausage after we had butchered, an egg in the spring, fruit pies when fresh fruit was in season.

At the end of the school day, at four o'clock, we waited for each other in front of Uncle Hirschler's notion store at the market place, and promptly started out for Geisberg. It was strictly forbidden to loiter in town, or even to linger in front of a store window. If one of us risked doing that, Mimi, our big sister and model, grabbed us by the sleeve and brought us back on the right trail. I enjoyed school. I had a good teacher and nice friends who remained the same throughout the seven years. I learned easily. But in 1911, after the examination at the end of primary studies, I had to stop school. That was hard!

In the meantime, things had changed at home. Aunt Suzanne had married and moved to Haut-Rhin. Aunt Madeleine lived in her own place at Geisberg. But, the worst of all was that Father was no longer living. Pneumonia had taken him on January 6, 1910, at the age of forty-seven years. He had been sick for only a few days. Grandmother's heart was broken by the loss of this, her only son; she died three months later. Grandfather, however, in spite of his old age, rallied and took over the management of the farm. Henry, my oldest brother, was fourteen years old and Jean (John), the youngest, only six months.

Six years later Grandfather died, at the age of eighty-one years. My mother bravely took up the responsibilities as head of the family, supported by my sister Mimi. She directed the farm with much skill and even succeeded to save enough money to buy one or two fields. Grandfather had died in the middle of the war, a time of scarce personnel and horses. The big brothers had been drafted. The girls had to do the heavy field work; often our backs would hurt. Sometimes women from the village or convalescing soldiers from the "Genesungskompanie" came to help us. We carried on as best as we could until the armistice and the return of our three brothers who were tired, starved, but unharmed.

Life returned to its normal course; we sowed and harvested, bought and sold. But in reality, everything was different. We had become French. That meant a hostile border separated us from our relatives, from our friends, and from two of our worship places—Haftelhof and Deutschhof. The Germans, our brothers in language and culture, had become our "enemies." The French, our former enemies, strangers whom we didn't understand, now had the authority over us. It was a painful chapter in our lives. With a heavy heart we had to conform.

We took French lessons in Wissembourg; then I decided to go to Paris. There was another reason for this. A certain young man had asked me for marriage and I wanted to take some distance to think about it. I found a family in Presles, a suburb of Paris, where I did housework from September 1919 to December 1920. That was a long time! From this Protestant couple, Hollard-Monod, and their six children, I learned a lot. Mr. Hollard was a professor at Sorbonne. They were joyful Christians. Their home was kept modestly and they consecrated all their means to help relieve the misery among the working class, orphans, and alcoholics.

On the advice of Madame Hollard, I visited museums and other historical sites in Paris. I was won over by the beauty, the charm, the elegance, and the majesty of these "French" works of art. My Sundays were spent at the center of the Association of Young Protestant Alsatians. I attended a German worship service and freely related to others of my countrymen. Invigorated by this touch from home, I returned to my work.

Finally, it was time to return home. I had made some progress in the French language. I could read simple books and hold a conversation. I had also accepted the marriage proposal. My sister Mimi was equally engaged to be married; we decided to celebrate our weddings the same day. Aunt Madeleine came to live with us for several weeks and together we prepared the necessary linens, trousseau, and clothing. My mother was not stingy about the expenses. Plans for the double wedding were made, and on April 14, 1921, Philipp Hege and I were married.

The following day my young husband came for me in a horse-drawn carriage to solemnly take me to my new home at Schafbusch. My mother-in-law, the four brothers-in-law and four sisters-in-law welcomed me warmly. They were younger than my husband and were eager to see what was going to happen.

So, now I belonged to this family which nine years earlier had created such a commotion when they took over the Schafbusch farm. It had been the subject of conversation in all the surrounding villages. Everything that Peter Hege undertook or purchased was noticed and was talked about and, if possible, imitated. The people at Geisberg were happy to have Mennonite neighbors and a minister. I remember my future father-in-law as a refined, cheerful man. One Sunday afternoon my sister and I asked him to teach us several new hymns from the book, *Frohe Botschaft*. He willingly sat down to the harmonium and we sang one hymn after another. I regretted his premature departure very much.

For more than ten years my mother-in-law continued to be in charge of the household. We did have a private living room, the "Abel Douay" room. It was difficult to be excluded when my husband discussed the affairs of the farm with his mother. In addition to what I brought along with my trousseau, as was the custom, my mother had given me a sum of money for my personal needs at the beginning. Later, I received a little spending money, the same as my brothers-in-law and my sisters-in-law. My mother-in-law did all the shopping, even buying the clothes for the children, always good quality but according to her own taste. She even bought the Christmas gifts, accompanied by my husband, without asking for my opinion. They were beautiful expensive gifts. So, to have something of my own to give I made small gifts with leftover materials and yarn that I found in the house. It was thirteen years later, after my mother-in-law retired, that the situation changed. About that time the government began family subsidy payments on a per-child basis.

I learned much from my mother-in-law. She was calm and firm and her sons were totally devoted to her. She confided in me in many things. She told me about her happy marriage. It was an arranged marriage by the parents. "But you will see," she said, "as you live together it gets better all the time." Actually, she had always known that her husband would not return from Russia; he had appeared to her briefly the night he died.

In later years I shared the household work with my sister-in-law Lydia, with whom I got along real well. The brothers and sisters of my husband had become my own. My mother kept her distance. She didn't understand the lifestyle of Schafbusch and rarely came to visit; my brothers and sisters even less. Mother lived with my brother Heinrich and his family. When I went to visit her it was not possible to have an intimate conversation with her. Contacts with a few personal friends became equally less and less frequent. On the other hand, Aunt Madeleine, an unmarried sister of my father, remained for me a friend until her death after the war. She sewed the clothes for the children and for myself, even the heavy corduroy outfits for the boys. Almost every year, in the spring and fall, she came to our house for several weeks.

Birth Of A Vocation

From notes of Great-Uncle Willy Hege, Boulay (November 1984)

One evening in November 1930, when everything was calm and quiet in the house, I was sitting alone at the dining room table when my sister-in-law Emma came and invited me to follow her for a talk in the Abel Douay room. This was the living room of my brother's family. It was unusual and I followed her, uneasy and self-conscious, asking myself what this could be all about. Philipp was not at home.

I stood in front of my sister-in-law, ready to listen respectfully. She explained that Aunt Madeleine was getting older and wanted to hand over the Sunday School to someone younger. She thought of me. I was nineteen years old and had never done anything like this before. I felt a weight coming down on me. But Emma encouraged me kindly: "Of course, you can do it. Just try it this coming Sunday. Here is a book which explains how to get children interested in Bible stories."

I remained standing and thought about it for a long time. I could not say, no; this is how the Sunday School teacher was born. I am still moved today when I remember that moment. Why me? Often I had taken an interest in my little nephews and nieces, such lovable little beings. On Sunday I took them on my knees, one after another, to page through the big illustrated Bible and told them stories from the Old and the New Testament. Surely, someone had observed this.

For a number of years I taught Sunday School, as long as I lived at Schafbusch. In the spring of 1937, I was ordained a minister at age twenty-five. I decided to go to the Chrischona Bible School to increase my knowledge of the Bible.

When I got married and moved to the farm of Salmiak, near Boulay (Moselle), I continued my service as a minister in the Diesen congregation.

Later, in 1949, I was ordained elder and today I am still in the service of the Lord. The beginning of this call—this is what I want to underscore—was this unusual conversation with my sister-in-law, Emma.

Dora, waits while the workers take a break to enjoy the refreshments she brought to them.

Dora,
Oldest Of The Philipp Hege Children, Remembers

I have memories of a happy childhood, of a regulated life with little that was unexpected, of established schedules during the week and on Sunday. Each season had its well-defined work, each day of the week precise chores, seasonal menus known in advance, but also, hours of rest. For the adults it was a peaceful life filled with hard work; for the scholars it meant hard studies, much homework, with little time for pleasure.

Just like our mother, we had to start at seven o'clock for the walk to school in Wissembourg. It never entered my father's mind to take us in the car in bad weather. We ate our lunch at school. We were not allowed to linger in front of store windows. Instead of walking the interesting market street, we were supposed to use a small alley where a little dog frightened me terribly. In spite of my fears, I would not have dared to disobey my mother. Discipline relaxed in later years, as it often happens in families and, to my astonishment, none of the brothers or sisters went astray.

As a whole, we were conscientious students who could be counted on. When I was only eight years old, my teacher sent me to the market to buy her vegetables. I was accompanied by a friend who chose the vegetables, but I held the money. At age twelve I regularly went between eleven o'clock and noon to pick up an envelope with cash, another teacher's salary. Later, my sister Irene had the same responsibility. For these services we were not paid, not even a little reward like some small advertising pictures of which the teacher had a whole drawer full. This was the normal thing.

Our mother tongue was Alsacian; our teachers had the difficult task to teach us French. It was expected of us to chat in French during recess under penalty of a written punishment. Often I preferred to keep quiet instead.

There were few books, no radio, and no record player at our house. We had to make our own music. Each of us took piano lessons with more or less enthusiasm. We seldom went away and seldom had company. We had no friendship relationships with people in the village, or schoolmates. We lived in two different worlds: the activities at school were French and life on the farm was Alsacian. We organized our own games among ourselves as brothers and sisters. As I got older I was sometimes bored. I thought nothing ever happened.

In 1937, we were fourteen children.

At the time when my parents were keeping house with my grandmother and the still unmarried uncles and aunts, there was in the "Sunday room" (it was closed during the week) a book shelf which contained, among others, an encyclopedia, *Brehms Tierleben*, in German, about the life of animals. There was also a big Bible illustrated by Schnorr von Carolsfeld, if my memory serves me right. On Sunday we were allowed to look at these if we were very careful. I was especially impressed with the illustrations of the prophet Daniel and the book of Revelation. Later that room became an extra bedroom.

At Christmas each adult and child received a plate of cookies and a book. also some handkerchiefs and a small object or toy. The book was never missing; it seemed a must. The adults received either stories of travel or biographies, or another "serious" book. Novels were prohibited. The children had books, adapted to their ages, which could be bought at the Evangelical bookstore in Strasbourg. Alas, before the end of vacation I had read all those accessible to me, and the year ahead was long. We also received something on our birthday, but never a gift during the year, neither candy nor chocolate. Our modest spending money had to be earned by the sweat of our brow during vacation by picking peas or currants or picking up potatoes.

I was twelve years old when Mother first confided in me that she was expecting a baby; it was number twelve. It was to be born in three months, she told me. I was honored that she trusted me with this secret and felt responsible to help her as much as possible. From the age of six I thought I understood that a certain commotion during the night had something to do with the birth of a new little brother or sister. So much so that at age seven I announced to my teacher the birth of a new baby, not able to specify the sex for the good reason that the little boy was born only several hours after I had left for school. It was the eighth child in the family.

After each birth Mother had to stay in bed for three days, lying quietly on her back. It was thought that this prevented blood clots. She was not allowed to go steps for nine days and had to stay upstairs. Only after three weeks did she again take up her usual activities. Special meals cooked in butter were prepared for her. Grandmother watched carefully over these. I remember the presence of a deaconess or nurse during these times. During the first days we were allowed to see Mother two or three times. On tiptoes we entered the room. Mother was resting peacefully and happily in her bed, the newborn sleeping in its crib. It was like a sanctuary.

The baby was changed at fixed hours so as not to disturb the schedule of the day. When he was older, he sat in a high chair at the table with us in the dining room while we were eating. But his turn came only after the

Father enjoyed taking our picture. Artfully, we were positioned in a variety of poses. Here the ten brothers stand according to age.

grown ups had eaten. While waiting, he played with his spoon or nibbled on a crust of bread. He amused us with his antics, but did not show the least bit of impatience. Mother had time to eat in peace and regain her strength. (Often the next baby was by then on the way.) Of course, Mother's days were filled with a good measure of work "well filled, taxing, and overflowing." Our parents seemed so happy with each new baby that we quite naturally were the same. At any rate, the parents adequately provided for the needs of each child. We had our own bed, our personal toys, and a private drawer to keep our things. Our clothes were well marked with our

View of experimental plots.

Father was forever measuring, counting, and evaluating his crops. The yield of this experimental plot was carefully measured. We children were sometimes included to give life to the experimental pictures.

initials; never would I have used a hanky, even a clean one, that did not have my initials on it.

It became more and more difficult to have an intimate conversation with Mother. I, as the oldest, had a privileged position, but several of my brothers and sisters suffered because of it. It must be emphasized that after 1939 the times were very hard and her task became practically super human.

Our parents were very different in nature. Mother was perceptive to beauty of all kinds: poetry, music, bird songs, and flowers. She knew how to put color into the grayest and most ordinary days. Shortly before her death, she confided in me that all her life she heard a soft melody within her. Not always the same, but always beautiful music. Father was a man of clarity, integrity, order, and punctuality. He needed the vast expanses of straight, flat, rectilinear fields to feel well. Those small hilly meadows at the far end of the property, which could not be leveled out, secretly irritated him to the end of his life. In spite of their differences, our parents were united. Mother would never have allowed anything against the wishes of our Father; but it was she who was the more flexible. It was through her that one had to maneuver to obtain a permission or a privilege. At times of important decisions in our lives we had a consultation with both of them. Mother watched for the right day and hour when Father was available. "Wait," she would say, "till the weekend is over; Father has the Sunday sermon to prepare!" At the right moment, in our presence, she presented the problem to him and, in a few well-chosen words, he gave us his counsel.

Father deeply loved his family, but he did not know how to show his feelings. He never sang or played with his children. He never took them in his arms. When we were sick, he came to see us, sometimes only on the second day. He had finally realized our absence at the table; or had Mother pointed it out to him? I still remember that he would sit down by our bed and ask us how we were feeling. With that, the conversation would stop. He finished by becoming absorbed in his thoughts or by pulling out a notebook from his pocket and taking down some notes. Finally, he left, a little embarrassed and almost relieved. But still, it made us feel good.

He enjoyed taking our pictures. Artfully, we were positioned by order of height, diagonally on the steps, sitting, standing, in Indian file, the girls and the boys separate, or all mixed up, while playing or ready to leave for school. Sometimes we were used to give life to shots of experimental fields, or some new installation on the farm which he wanted to photograph.

Twice a year, on Saturday evening, Father appeared in the bathroom with his big ruler and the farm scale in order to measure us, weigh us, and record the results in a carefully kept little notebook. He compared the figures obtained with the ones from the last time, did some adding and subtracting, and calculated the averages and the totals. One of us had grown a lot, another hardly "budged." In total, his children had gained X kilos, grown Y centimeters, which made an average of so much. Here, at least, were results that could be calculated. For this is what Father enjoyed doing—anything that had to do with calculations.

Father was forever measuring, counting, evaluating his crops, his expenses, his profits, etc.... This was not uniquely because of the imperatives of profitability and the necessity to feed his large family, but also his love for mathematics and a desire to constantly surpass himself.

There was an atmosphere of respect in the family and a submission to the Word of God. There was no swearing by any of the adults, neither by grandmother, nor the parents, uncles or aunts, no rudeness or insult, no doubtful jokes or lies. Every day, after the evening meal, Father read a passage from the Bible. Sunday was a sacred day of rest; farm work was limited to the care of the animals and no field work was done, no matter what the weather was like. The whole family, adults and children, went to church in the morning. In the afternoon the children met for Sunday School or religious instruction according to their ages. In the evening at dusk Mother gathered us around her to sing the beautiful hymns from the *Singvögelein*, the collection of songs for Sunday Schools from the German Baptist Church. We especially enjoyed singing the many Christmas songs. She spoke little of her faith, but the fervor with which she sang communicated without words the certainty of an invisible reality of her love for the Almighty. In general, there reigned a spirit of piety, of peace, and contentment in the home which marked us deeply. All of us have chosen to follow God and our Savior Jesus Christ in the same way. However, when it was time to leave the parental home to enter the real world and stand on our own feet, it was a shock.

Did I paint a gloomy and harsh picture of our childhood? It wasn't that way at all. We all have happy memories. The discipline had nothing oppressive. It provided a safe frame which allowed for the unfolding of happiness and a love for life, shared and multiplied joys, and an atmosphere of laughter about anything and nothing.

In this way the years passed until September 1, 1939, the day when all the people of the border zone, where we lived, were evacuated and when the war threw our family into a whirlwind. We were thrown from right to left; from Schafbusch to the Haute-Vienne (central France) and back again; then from Schafbusch to Heilbronn (Germany); and finally returned home. We experienced all kinds of anxieties and privations. A member of the family lost his life. The French, the Germans, and again the French questioned us, suspecting us to be spies or accusing us of treason. We were harassed again and again with deportation and internment. Finally, after the armistice, we returned to our farm which lay in ruins and had been plundered, at the very last, of almost all our goods. But we were happy to find our "home" and were ready to rebuild again.

During the War of 1939-1945

"Thus says the Lord: I am going to break down what I built and pluck up what I planted, that is the whole land. And you seek great things for yourself? Do not seek them; for I am going to bring disaster upon all flesh, says the Lord, but I will give you your life as a prize of war in every place to which you may go." Jeremiah 45: 4-5

Evacuation to the Haute-Vienne (South France) And Our Sojourn There

For the Alsace the hardship of war began before the declaration of the war on September 1, 1939. A few hours after Hitler's army marched into Poland, the chief executive of the French army ordered the immediate evacuation of 380,000 persons. One hundred and fifty towns and villages, the region between the Rhine and the Maginot Line (including the city of Strasbourg) were to be completely emptied. Their inhabitants evacutated to the southwest of France. Secretly held preparations had been made by the government since 1935. History books tell nothing about this. Here, however, follows a report of our personal experience.

Father: In 1939 the harvest is late and by the end of August we just finish bringing in and threshing the last wheat when, on September 1, we need to say good-bye to house and farm. War threatens and the French government gives the order to evacuate the ten-mile strip between the French Maginot Line and the German Siegfried Line where we live. Quickly, we prepare two wagons, pulled by a pair of horses each, covered with a tarp. These are loaded with all kinds of household goods which seem important: clothes, bedding, food, and other items. We also take a cow, which soon becomes exhausted, and we abandon her at the side of the road. I take my wife and the four youngest children in our car and drive to the Kälberbruch near Winterhausen where we know a family by the name of Eyer. My wife and children stay there while I go back as far as Schönenbourg to meet up with the others. We spend the night in a barn together with the families from Geisberg.

Mother: It is evening, the end of a long, hot summer day. I just put my four youngest children to sleep on the mattresses and blankets in a room upstairs, made available by the farmer's wife. I, too, lay down and reflect on the eventful day.

In the morning we made bread dough and baked thirty loaves of bread, eighteen mirabelle pies, besides making a special meal for the army officers stationed in our house. The farm is teeming with soldiers. From the barn comes the sound of the threshing machine which is threshing the last of the wheat. An overwhelming fear hangs in the air. Is there going to be war? If yes, will we need to leave as the rumors go? At four in the afternoon the phone rings. We must leave. We are told to take provisions for three days, also blankets and clothes, and be on the road within two hours. Already there is heavy traffic—busses, military vehicles, farmers' wagons loaded with bundles of clothes, bedding, food baskets, and feed for the draft animals. On top of the baggage sits the family, children, and old people. They come from the mountain village behind Wissembourg. Some have only one cow to pull the wagon and the calf is tied to the back. The train of vehicles is endless.

We pack. I give instructions; the older children help in making selections. Shall we take the baby clothes along for the soon expected child? (Mother is eight months pregnant and does not know that she will have twins.) The smaller ones who have never traveled before are excited about the unusual activities. "May we go along too?" they ask. For a last time we gather around the big dining table. Father reads a psalm and prays with us.

It is six o'clock and we leave the farm, leaving everything behind: the animals (cows, calves, pigs, and chickens); the garden full of vegetables; luscious fruit (apples, pears, peaches, mirabelles, and plums); all the reserves for winter. But, mostly our comfortable home where we have been so happy. Already the soldiers take over. Without looking back we take our place in the long line of refugees.

From side streets other traffic joins in. This causes congestion and the column moves more slowly all the time. Here a team had stopped because an exhausted calf fell over. There a sick grandfather sits by the roadside. But we must continue on our way, on and on.... We take a side road in our car and Father drops us off at an isolated farm, far from all the turmoil.

For the moment all is quiet; but the questions about the rest of the family haunt me. Have Father and the ten older children found a shelter for the night? What is going to happen to us? But then a verse of psalm comes to my mind: "I will both lie down and sleep in peace; for you alone, O Lord, make me lie down in safety." - Psalm 4:8. And a peace beyond understanding fills my soul.

Some of the Geisberg Mennonite community pause for a photo during one of the stops along the way to evacuation from their homes. On the left with the white cane is blind Daniel Hirschler.

Father: The following day, Saturday, all the families of Geisberg and Schafbusch meet at the Kälberbruch. We spend a peaceful Sunday in fellowship and have an open-air worship service. Right away on Monday morning we need to separate since the families from Geisberg must stay with the community of Altenstadt, whereas we from Schafbusch will join the families from Steinseltz. Our destination is the train station of Marmoutier.

Dora: For ten days, our two teams travel west toward Marmoutier in sunshine and rain in the endless refugee stream. We spend the nights in villages, sleeping on hay or straw. Some farmers receive us kindly, others with mistrust. We are never free from fear of an air attack, but nothing like that happens.

Father: I take my wife and the small children to Wasselone where we ask an Eyer family to take us in. We stay there for a few days until the freight train, which is to transport our community, arrives at the train station in Marmoutier. The residents from Schafbusch, family and employees numbering twenty-seven people, with all their belongings, fill up one freight car. Finally, on September 11, the endless long train sets in

Some of the Geisberg and Schafbusch families pose in front of the Hege farm wagons at the Mennonite farm of Kälberbruch.

motion—into uncertainty. Besides the four employees, my brother Otto and his wife Dina, with their five small boys—René, André, Jean, Herrmann, and Daniel—are also with us. Three other laborers remained in the Alsace since their village was not evacuated. The four Polish workers, two men and two women, will leave us after we get to our destination.

Mother: As best as we can we stack our sacks, bundles, mattresses, blankets, and food provisions, and make ourselves as comfortable as possible. The children are filled with wonder at the scenery which passes in front of our eyes: cities, villages, meadows, and woods. The older girls and I bring out some knitting; we sing; sometines we shed a tear. The hours slip by. As the sun sets, we share a bite to eat, light the old barn lantern, and fasten it to the ceiling. Each makes himself comfortable for the night as best as he can and we fall asleep to the regular tac-tacatac, tac-tacatac sound of our train. A freight car has no shock absorbers....

At midnight I awake with a start. An event is about to begin! In a quiet voice I awaken Father. The train rolls on and on. If only it would come to a stop! Dora, our oldest (Father speaks only limited French), tries to get the attention of the train conductor. By a miracle we are in the first car! Finally, the train slows down and we stop at a small train station. Now everything goes real fast! Dora has already found a doctor and leads him to our boxcar. Finally, help is here!

The doctor arrives just in time to deliver a small girl. Then he exclaims, "Well, here comes another one!" Forty-five minutes after the arrival of the doctor I held two precious babies in my arms—a girl and a boy. But, we must get to a hospital as quickly as possible. The baby clothes cannot be located; someone finds a sheet in which we wrap the two newborns. I am placed on a stretcher on the platform. Father steps close to me for a last time. He has to stay with the rest of the family and continue the trip without giving us an address. We quickly decide on the names, Martha and Théo, and say good-bye. It is September 12, 1939. I am confident; I know I am in God's hand. Above me there is a beautiful starry sky. Dora is next to me with the precious bundle in her arms. My oldest daughter will stay with me; the doctor decided it this way.

Why did this train, which had been traveling for hours without stopping even once, suddenly develop problems and have to interrupt the journey just at the moment when it was most critical for me? Yes, our Heavenly Father can use some very ordinary ways to help us in a time of need.

Father: The following morning we continue our trip, after we moved from our defective boxcar into another one. We reach Limoges (Haute-Vienne, South France), then Le Dorat, and finally Oradour-Saint-Genest. Almost the whole village of Steinseltz is housed here and our family is assigned an old dilapidated mill outside of town.

Dora: Mother and I are in Sézanne near Paris. An ambulance brought us here to the hospital. In reality it is an old cloister which is a home for elderly women. It also has a hospital ward with a modest operating room, and a maternity ward with three or four beds. The maternity ward has a door leading to an inner courtyard where the

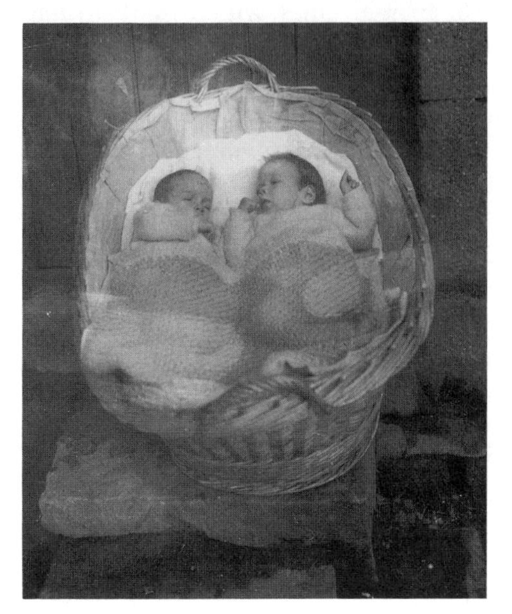

The twins rest in their basket. Théo and Martha were born on the train at the train stop in Sézanne.

Mother, the twins and Dora were taken to this hospital in Sézanne.

cold water spigot is located. The nuns are as self-giving as they are poor. The meals are meager and highly spiced. They consist mostly of cabbage, dry beans, and lentils. The food does not agree well with Mother and she suffers from it for months afterwards.

I am assigned a bed in the primitive dormitory with the old women. Those that are bedfast are being cared for by the healthier ones; the others pass the day sitting side by side on benches in the dining hall along the three walls. Idle, with an empty look, they wait for death. I am very touched. Titina, the nurse and night watch, sleeps in the room with Mother, who is the only maternity patient at the present. Titina is a deaf mute. To alert her at night, one has to pull a string which is fastened to her wrist. The midwife is an impressive personality of average build, with eyes of striking forget-me-not color. She radiates confidence and vitality.

Eagerly, the midwife told us that of all the French midwives, she held the record for the most deliveries and was to receive a designation from the President. She shows us the beautiful hat that she has already bought for the occasion. It is decorated with a bird of paradise feather. In the meantime, the war started and the hat remains in the closet. Her methods, however, are quite old fashioned. The infants have their diapers changed only twice each day and are wrapped the old-fashioned way—legs wrapped together tightly as straight as possible, arms so they can't move, held against the sides with a scarf, which is crossed over the chest rather firmly. The head and hands are the only parts that can move. Sometimes Mother tries to loosen the strong bands, but only secretly. She doesn't want to offend the best midwife of France. We observe all this with amazement.

Fortunately, cow's milk agrees with our premature twins; however, they are very sleepy and we spend hours feeding them. What time I have to spare, I spend in making baby clothes. Just three months ago I took my exams to enter the Teachers College, and I still remember the sewing course. I remember the patterns for shirts, sacks, bibs, and diapers; even the exact measurements. By memory I can knit baby sweaters. The house master of the cloister bought two balls of wool (one pink and the other blue), and a wash basket made of willows. It was the last one he could find in Sézanne. Since the declaration of the war, people crowd the stores and the reserves are depleted. Besides, we have very little money. Mother Superior allows us to have some used sheets. We line the wash basket and prepare it as a traveling bed. We thankfully receive other precious gifts; however, I don't remember from whom.

Mother: The elderly doctor kindly cares for us. He even brings visitors from Alsace. They are railway men who were transferred to Sézanne. Slowly, I regain my strength. Finally, we get a letter from our loved ones. They located in the area of Limoges and are doing well. This gives us courage, and after two weeks nothing and no one can hold us back. We want to join the rest of our family.

Dora: We had planned to travel during the night; however, we miss our connection to Limoges in Paris in the evening due to the neglect of the Red Cross driver who was to take us from one train station to the other. The twins and our baggage, put on the train by zealous boy scouts, almost leaves without us. We are forced to spend the night in the waiting room at the train station. Little Théo cries and cries. Only towards morning is he given a bottle. The following day—it is my seventeenth birthday—an old gentleman, a Red Cross volunteer, comes to help us. He helps us board the train into second class, even though our tickets are for third class. He leaves and is soon back again with a morning newspaper and some candy for my birthday. This unexpected attention amply compensates for the humiliations endured the past two weeks.

Mother: Now we are traveling to the south. The scenery changes, and it is more and more rugged—uncultivated fields, neglected areas, undergrowth, poor villages, and houses in ruins. Everything is different. A private car takes us to our destination: Oradour-Saint-Genest. The whole family is gathered and welcomes us. Father and the children are all in good health—Ernest, Irène, Alfred, René, Eric, Erica, Willy, Fritz, Uli, Alice, Oscar, Hans, and Louise. What a gift!

But, what about our housing! It is a run-down mill beside a stream which is no longer occupied because of the risk of falling down! A cracked outside wall is propped up. It is not very kind of the owner to make such a house available to us. The only decent room, a wash kitchen on the ground floor, remains locked to us as long as we live there. The owner comes daily and counts the few spotted peaches which ripen in his pitiful garden; our children are amused. When we go to bed, mattresses are laid side by side on the floor. There, I hear a noise. It is a rat! It comes closer. Then it is frightened and disappears. This is not very reassuring!

In the morning we wash ourselves by the stream; there is no running water or drain in the house, or any other toilet facility. However, there are plenty of bushes all around.... There is drinking water in a hole in the middle of a pasture about 500 meters distance. Early in the morning the older children take all available containers to fill them with water at this hole before the cattle come to drink and make it dirty. We also need milk. Here and there graze a few skinny cows. The farmers milk them only when they need milk.

We are living in a different world. News of our arrival spreads. The curious come and want to see the twins. Some pity us, others admire us. They bring us children's clothes, diapers, and even a sheet. The mayor comes in person carrying wool blankets. We also receive several camping beds and a small stove, 50cm in diameter, for cooking and for heating water. Representatives of several relief agencies, from France and abroad, alternately come to our door. They all agree: "Your situation is not very good here," and leave again.

Excerpts of Father's Letter From the Haute-Vienne:

Among the papers of Pierre Sommer from Montbéliard, the editor of the monthly Mennonite paper, *Christ Seul,* were several letters from Philipp Hege, written in the Haute-Vienne in inner France where the family was living in temporary shelters. A few excerpts follow:

Oradour-St.-Genest, October 3, 1939

...Dear Brother Sommer,

A few days ago my wife with Dora and the twins arrived here safely and now my whole large family is reunited in very tight quarters. Our situation is bearable and yet much has to improve before winter.... We very much miss our Christian literature. Well, we do have our Bible and we understand some things so much better. The daily readings, too, often give us much comfort. May God grant that we understand His word to us and that this present time can become a blessing for us as children of God. We are released from our earthly homes.... I had often feared whether I could give up my earthly belongings for the sake of Christ. Today I still have my wife and my 16 children who are all adjusting to our situation and this makes it a lot easier. Should I lose my family for the sake of Christ, then God will also provide the necessary strength....

We would welcome a visit of one or two German-speaking Mennonite ministers, in spite of the great distance.

(There follows a list of addresses of families from the Geisberg congregation.)

Would it be possible to publish a list in Christ Seul, *since other families from Lorraine and Upper Alsace also had to leave their homes?*

Father: Very soon the Polish workers leave us and my brother Otto's family finds another shelter. Since he has German nationality he is temporarily interned. Gradually, as best as we can, with the few things at our disposal, we get used to the new living conditions in this poor and primitive region. Our car stayed in the Alsace; however, we have several bicycles, and I re-learn riding a bike. In this way I can visit the families

Father's brother, Otto, and his family at their temporary refugee home.

from Geisberg from time to time. They live at some distance from us in this region, in Lussac, and in other places.

Mother: The two oldest daughters live in boarding school: Irène in Capbreton, where her school from Strasbourg was relocated; Dora in Périgueux in the also relocated teachers' college. That means two persons less to lodge. Ernest, at sixteen, works for a farmer; and Alfred, fourteen, next to Father, is my main support. He helps everywhere. He cuts up wood at the edge of the stream, does laundry, cleans the house, gets water and milk. Seven of the younger children go to school in the village.

Dora: Irène and I had teachers in Wissembourg who encouraged us to continue our education to the "top," which means to the entrance exam for the teachers' college. Whereas, our brothers had teachers who made fun of high school students to the point of discouraging education beyond grade school. This is the reason why the boys helped with housework and the girls were left to continue their studies.

Mother: Fall brings fog, rain, and cold. The children crowd around the stove which lacks dry firewood. Doing laundry poses a problem. It is still possible to wash in the stream, but where can we dry the laundry and the many diapers? I am ready to despair. Then comes a call from the window below. Two women refugees who work in the soup kitchen offer to dry my laundry near the stove, as long as the soup kitchen is in operation. This is a sign, among many others, that our Heavenly Father does not forget us.

Following is another excerpt of Father's letters from the Haute-Vienne:

Oradour-St.-Genest, November 27, 1939

...Things are going well and many situations have improved since my last letter. We now have a small stove, electric lights, and also a little more room.... As I indicated earlier, I had returned home to the Alsace in October. I was able to pack some things and bring them to safety.... Some of my books are here with me now; they give me some reading material. It was very uncomfortable at home; it was unfriendly.... Some day, when we return home, a big job is waiting for us; to bring everything back to normal. Well, for the time being I am not worrying about this, and place it all in God's hand. He will do all things well. Through these events we have been detached from so much. We well know that we are looking forward to a heavenly inheritance. How comforting it is for us to know that the

Lord will soon return. In light of this the future looks very simple, especially when I think of my large family. Today it is the same as it was before the children of Israel left Egypt. For the Egyptians (the children of the world) it was dark; for the people of Israel (the children of God) it was light....

Yesterday we were able to meet with the families of Geisberg in Les Bouiges and we celebrated communion together. We felt the Lord's blessing and presence in a very special way.

(On this occasion there was an offering of 2,500frs and there followed instructions on how this money was to be sent to the mission in Java, and it was to be recorded in *Christ Seul* as "anonymous" [underlined]. During this time each adult refugee received 9frs per day from the State and each child, 5.5frs.)

Father: By the end of October the enemies have not yet reached our borders. Our mayor, Georges Rupp, decides to travel to the Alsace with a group and invites me to go along. We travel by car. I don't recognize Schafbusch anymore. The stables are empty; some farm machines are missing; granaries and barns are equally empty. On one of the doors of the granary there is a greeting to the owner written in chalk. There is not much missing in the house itself, with the exception of the costly silverware from my mother. There is a signed voucher by the commander of Wissembourg in its place. He is the one who prevented looting at the beginning, but then was transferred. My office was rummaged through; also the drawer which had the photo negatives. The courtyard buzzes with soldiers. They invite me to eat with them. An officer questions me since I am not accompanied by the police. A petty officer from Wissembourg, Philipp Young, whom I know (he belongs to the Chrischona congregation), helps me fill some suitcases and boxes with clothes. I take my wife's glasses, her sewing basket, and her sewing machine. The next day I load this baggage on a trailer which I borrow from Veitinger in Soultz. Then I am stopped, accused of spying, and tried in Morsbronn, but finally released. Now I can load my possessions into a train compartment. I continue to Wasselone to the Eyer family. There I can regain my strength before taking my train back to the Haute-Vienne. My loved ones welcome me with relief, because news had spread that I had been arrested in the Alsace.

Mother: For the first of Advent we decorate the walls of our rooms with green branches since there are no pine trees. We sing Advent and Christmas songs, one after another, which makes quite an impression on one of the many Red Cross representatives who stops by.

Mother does the laundry in front of the house at Oradour. Note the cracked wall on the house.

Dora: The following newspaper article—I do not know the name of the paper—was prompted by this "scene." Father had collected several French and foreign newspaper articles which report about our family. There are two which we found.

Newspaper Article 1939—"I Look Outside"

The Little Gironde, the daily newspaper from Bordeaux, has an article about the Alsacians who found refuge in some regions of southwest France. Several paragraphs appear here:

Suddenly pulled out from everything which made up their lives and transplanted into regions which are unfamiliar to most—often lacking the most basic things—these refugees from Alsace and Lorraine deserve our respect.

Many of them bear with an admirable courage this total upheaval of their lives. For example, there is the case of a family made up of a father, mother, and sixteen children. Before the war they were a well-to-do farming family, owners of a large model farm in the region of Wissembourg. Within a few months they lost everything: house and farm buildings, animals and farm equipment. At present they live in an old abandoned mill near Limoges. They are crowded into three rooms, two of which are used for bedrooms where eight boys sleep on straw. Four beds are shared by the rest of the family.

The oldest of the sixteen children is seventeen. The youngest, twins, were born on the freight train between the Alsace and Paris. They are now contentedly lying side by side in a wash basket. They get their daily bath in a washtub. All the children are healthy, rosy, blond, and clean; and there reigns a surprising serenity and joy of life in this old abandoned mill.

A social worker visited them to find out what the family needs. She describes their situation: "The mother, a 40-year-old peasant woman, declares, 'When it is too sad inside, I look out the window; it is so beautiful outside.'"

• • •

What a good lesson this brave woman teaches us at a time when there is nothing good to be seen in the old European mill. Nature outside is so beautiful and divine, that it is worth the effort to look away from the unhappy circumstance in which we find ourselves from time to time, to the beauty of God's nature.

There are circumstances where it seems hard not to sigh and complain. But this does not take away the painful situation. Whoever can pull away from contemplating their misery and turn their thoughts to the source of eternal comfort will certainly benefit from it. They will discover there a new freedom which cannot be taken away by trials that are common to human kind. These efforts often direct us into better conditions.

In this way we begin to see life from a better side, because the outlook has been directed to eternal values and spiritual beauties. HIERATUS

Mother: On Sunday we attend the evangelical service which was organized for the refugees in the Catholic village of Oradour. This is comforting! Our twins are still in the narrow wash basket where they warm each other. This is a good thing because it is cold. Under the bed of the four other little ones an icicle has formed. Those little ones are from two to six years old and sleep three lengthwise and one across the bottom. The twins do not make normal progress. Little Théo is especially pale and thin. He has wrinkles in his face like an old man. The conditions are really too primitive and miserable in this mill. Once more a social worker confirms this and promises to help us. Then it is Christmas! We receive many packages from friends, known and unknown: food, clothes, and toys. There is hardly enough room to store it all.

But in January our social worker, Mademoiselle Monod, finally finds something for us; sixty kilometers from here in the small mountain village of La Jonchère. She takes the parents along to take a look at the modest and clean little house. Compared with our present place, it is a real castle! It is situated on the side of the mountain out in the country. And we move. We need a large vehicle for the family and a small one for the furniture and baggage. Ice and snow do not bother us. Hope gives us wings and we are not disappointed. Ten minutes from our future

An English newspaper dated April 3, 1940, featured the Hege family who had responded with gratitude for the relief goods that they had received.

home we stop at the home of a retired couple, Mr. and Mrs. Bonnaud. They receive us warmly. The older children help to clean the house and get it ready to move in. The name of our new home is called "The Buisson." There is a bedroom for the girls, two for the boys, one for the parents with the little ones; a kitchen fully equipped, including running water, and a sink with a drain. It also has a dining room where we set up a big table and simple benches. Enough room, finally! And what a beautiful view! Valleys and hills as far as the eye can see. In the east is a mountain range which reminds us of Schafbusch. What a treat!

Father writes:

At the Buisson, Poste office La Jonchére, Haute-Vienne
February 5, 1940.

...It is two weeks now that we are living here, all alone on a farm at 500m altitude. We decided to move, since we have more space here; all the farm buildings are available to us. We have a garden, field, meadow, pasture, woods.... It takes the children 20 minutes to walk to school. Our neighbors are very friendly and ready to help.... We have much reason to be thankful. God has put a special burden on us, but He also

helps in His own special way.... We also received some furniture: new wardrobes, tables, chairs, and beds. Such furniture had almost become unknown to us.... Being thankful makes the disagreeable easier to bear, and God keeps giving us more and more reasons to thank Him. Of course, there are other moments, too, when one wants to despair, where it is hard to submit to the will of God. But then God gives new strength again, as we turn to Him. How differently God's word speaks to us today than in earlier days when, because of so much work, it was hard to find the time to read. This difficult time is becoming a time of blessing to us. He is in control of all things....

Unfortunately, I am now further from the other Geisberg families (70-80km), so it is more difficult to get together without the use of a car. We had hoped to bring the others here, also, but in the meantime the houses were occupied or proved to be too small.

Mother: The owner of the "Buisson," a doctor, provides us with a cow which gives lots of milk. We call her "Negro." Alfred no longer has to walk for miles for just a small can of milk. Spring is coming. We clean up the square, cemented laundry basin outside which is fed by a clear spring. We put up a washline. Finally our laundry gets nice and clean again! Each day Father walks to the village of La Jonchère, with the big backpack, to get groceries. He speaks very little French, but always manages to get what we need. He thinks of everything, even the chocolate for our four o'clock snack. The children go to school in La Jonchère. Ernest and Alfred split wood and, with the neighbor's old white horse, plow a piece of land for a future vegetable garden.

Father: My sister Lydia lives nearby. She is a widow with four daughters—Louise, Hélène, Emma, Agnes—and is caring for two foster boys, Jean-Pierre and Gilbert. Each Sunday the two families meet for a worship service.

Father's sister Lydia and her family. Standing from left: daughters Emma, Helene, Louise, and Agnes. Seated from left, foster boys Jean-Pierre and Gilbert.

March 25. *Our flourishing congregation is widely scattered. If only this time can be a blessing to the individual; maybe, someday we can all be reunited at "home." The most important for us is our eternal home and peace in our hearts....*

(At this time there is again mention of a gift of 500fr, to be recorded under "anonymous." Of this gift, 200fr is designated for the mission in Java.)

Some time ago I received a letter from our missionary Klassen, which brought much joy to me.... The hardest thing for me here is that I miss the fellowship with other ministers.... Through letters from my sister we learned that Conference was held in Ludwigshafen as usual; also, that the Bible conferences were held at Thomashof. I fear that if things continue as they are, hard times are ahead for our congregations there. Shall we fear the future of the anti Christ? Shouldn't we rather rejoice in Christ?

June 14, 1940. *...From what we hear, Schafbusch and Geisberg are reported to be destroyed. Therefore, another earthly support is taken away. How good it is when we can put our complete trust in the Lord, and to have learned and still learn that all is well, no matter what happens.*

I read in the Mennonitischen Rundschau *publication that the Americans are doing relief work among the Spanish refugees in France. The thought came to me if it wouldn't be a good idea for these American organizations to have the addresses of the Mennonite refugees who are currently in this area. Right now there is probably no one in dire need, but we don't know if this could change.*

We want to continue to remember each other in prayer. With warm greetings, *Philipp Hege and family*

Mother: All is peaceful. We are content to be by ourselves in this beautiful countryside without business worries and employees. Our twins are doing better. Each has received their own bed from the social worker, Mademoiselle Monod... one pink, the other blue. Baby laundry "blows in the breezes" on all sides of the house. Now, since Father gives them orange juice daily and that they get out in the fresh air and sun, they visibly thrive. They are surrounded and spoiled by their many brothers and sisters. Of course, I can hardly keep after my many tasks; but, I am encouraged by the many improvements. How I enjoy doing the laundry outside when the sky is blue, as nature awakes and a multitude of birds sing and chirp in the nearby woods! Our devoted neighbor lady stops by several times a week to inquire of our needs and to admire our progress.

The director of the teachers' college where Dora is studying furnished us with a new kitchen stove and many other things we needed. With the arrival of summer comes vacation time and both older daughters return home. We enjoy the happy activities around us. The boys play in an abandoned quarry across the road. They build cabins and observe the birds. The girls help with the cooking, washing, mending, and do knitting. Huckleberries ripen in the woods. The people from the area show no interest in them; therefore, our children gather large quantities. We make pies and jam and eat them stewed. We are so privileged! In other parts of the world there is war with all the misery, distress, and upheavel that goes with it. Germany has invaded France. New refugees arrive in the village. Bread is getting scarce. Fortunately, we can now harvest potatoes and vegetables from our garden. We receive news from the Alsace: German troops occupy the territory. Friends come to visit and we discuss the situation.

Excerpts of letters Mother wrote from "Le Buisson"
to her mother who lived with a son and his family about sixty miles away

La Jonchère, at "Le Buission," February 29, 1940:

...We are glad that the cold weather is over; the warm sun feels good. I am renewed with courage. Thank God, we are all well. Some of the children had to be in bed for awhile, some are still coughing. René has to miss school now and then; he has grown so fast. Our little twins have made good progress. They can now raise their heads and are always pleasant; it is a joy to care for them. Slowly life is becoming more settled. We have whitewashed three rooms; it looks more friendly this way. We cook in the kitchen downstairs; we have received a nice small stove. I hope the oven works. I would so much like to bake a cake. Since we left Schafbusch this has not been possible. It is impossible to buy fresh vegetables. Our carrots are all used up by now....

My days are filled with cooking and washing, taking care of the children, and mending. I am just glad when I can get the most important things done. But, there are many improvements from Oradour. Since last week we have a cow, a Hollander, which is grazing in the meadow nearby. In a few weeks there will be a calf and then we can begin milking. In the meantime, we look forward to the Easter vacation. We expect Dora to come home, but don't know about Irène. Irène left last week for Capbreton near Spain to a school relocated from Strasbourg which opened on February 1. We don't know if they have Easter vacation, but it would be hard if Irène could not come; she is still so young....

"Le Buisson," April 24, 1940:

...My days are so busy, before I know it one week after another has gone by. We had three warm days, but since Monday the weather is cool and cloudy. In the garden things grow only slowly; we have flea beetles and snails; some things had to be sowed the second time. Right now cherry trees are in bloom, but they are only wild ones. The children look forward to them anyhow. In the meadow in front of the house countless blue hyacinths are blooming. They smell like the ones in the garden. Early in the morning there is a bird concert; the familiar birds from home. A cuckoo bird seems to have a nest nearby, and in the evening the frogs take their turn. This gives variety.

Thank God we are all in good health, the big ones and the little ones. For Easter we were all together. Irène could be with us for two weeks, but they went by so fast. We had to get summer clothes ready for her since we don't expect to see her again before July or August. This seems like a long time! Irène is still so young. They get very good care and she is doing well. Dora is not quite as far away. We hope to see her at Pentecost. Ernest and Alfred have plenty to do. They help with the housework, take care of the cow, and do the milking. We have plenty of milk for ourselves and Lydia.

There is always wood to cut. We can help ourselves to all we need in the woods nearby.

...René, Eric, and Willy go the French school; the others go to a refugee school. They have school all day. Some take lunch along; some come home to eat. For myself, I never leave the house. Philipp does all the shopping. I am glad; it would take too much of my time. The school boys bring the bread home each day. It is also heavy to carry. We seldom get visitors up here. You can see what the twins look like on the picture. This is the way they looked at Easter. They give us so much joy, but naturally, also some work. But, everything is so much easier here than in Oradour. Little Louise is a loving happy child, giving us lots of entertainment. Hans was for a time so pale, but looks better now.

...When will it be that we can all go to our home again?

"Le Buisson," June 14, 1940:

...The whole situation has not improved since my last letter. It is hard to be cheerful and our thoughts are with the many out there who are in danger. Now there is also the distress with the many refugees. Where will this end? From the Hege brothers there is good news, but they are both in dangerous positions....We have not heard anything from Aunt Madeleine. We are half afraid that she had to flee again. That would be hard, especially since she was so well cared for there. One has to wonder where it is safe to be. Here at the Buisson we live peacefully. For weeks the only stranger who comes up here is the mailman. Thank God, we are mostly all in good health; only Fritz is in bed since Monday with measles, rather high fever, racking cough, but already is getting better. The spots are less red today. I have some Homeopathic medicine. I have been glad for that more than once. You don't call a doctor very quickly here. We can expect more of the children to come down with measles since all those younger then Fritz have not had them. We will wait and see! ...Last week Willy, Fritz, Uli, and Alice had to be vaccinated, also Philipp and I. All the schools are closed. We hardly know what will happen next. We don't know if Dora and Irene will come home now too. Irène was to take her exams next week. We look forward to the time when we can all be together again. The twins are quite lively and happy, but in comparison to the others of the same age, they are slower. Most of the time they lie down, and can only sit for a short time. We are so happy that we are privileged to have them.

...Here in our garden things are growing now. We notice that we are in a higher elevation; it takes longer than in the Alsace. We are happy that we may grow something.

"Le Buisson," June 29, 1940:

...Finally, yesterday we got a letter form Irène. She passed her exam and will come as soon as the trains run again. It is so very far from here! Dora is still in Périgueux. She can come too, as soon as there is a train. ...Uli, Oscar, and Louise have the measles. The boys are almost over them, but little Louise is very sick. It hurts to see her. Otherwise, all is well. The twins are lively. We have many huckleberries here; this is a welcome treat.

The war has ended now; but for us, many difficulties still lie ahead. God gives us a burden, but He also helps us.

"Le Buisson," July 19, 1940:

Thank you for your last letter. It was an interruption from all the waiting in the last weeks....We finally received a letter from Willy. He is in captivity and is all right. He does not write where he is; also, no address. Therefore, we cannot write to him, but we are glad to know that he is alive. ...Gradually, old letters are coming from the Alsace. Maybe, there will soon be a change; so far we are not hearing anything. The refugees in the village don't know anything. We heard that some men from Wissembourg have returned to the Alsace to see what it looks like there. We are anxious to hear, and it is hard to know what to believe of all the talk. Finally, our big girls have come home, both unannounced. On Thursday afternoon Dora came slinking in, and this morning the kitchen door opened suddenly and Irène stuck her head in. What joy that was! It is good that they could come home. Food is getting scarce in these schools. We feel sorry for the many other girls who had to stay because they could not travel to their parents in the Alsace. They are also not able to get mail from their parents. Irène saw many German soldiers. They march through the streets and sing at the top of their voices....We are all in good health again. Eight of our children had the measles, some pretty bad.

"Le Buisson," August 1, 1940:

...Oscar has not yet been released. Maybe in another week, if he is fortunate. Then we hope he can come here. It is wearing; we had hoped it would go faster with the release. On Sunday a week ago Lydia Hirschler came from Limoges. We were happy to see her again. She came early in the morning and could stay for the night. She had many things to tell us.... We hear that in the village of Ingolsheim many houses are destroyed; temporary barracks are being built. We have many more questions but we have to be patient. What do you hear from Altenstadt? Did the mayor

also go to check things out? Here in La Jonchère we feel relieved. The 300 refugees from Paris have left. Maybe it will be easier to buy food now. In July we could get sugar for only three on our eighteen rationing cards. We eat mainly potatoes now and all kinds of vegetables from our "plantation." By now it is all doing well. What a blessing! The huckleberries are coming to an end. We benefited greatly. Too bad sugar was so scarce. One could have taken greater advantage. We are buying a lot of tomatoes, 5 frs the kg; up here in our altitude they are slow to ripen. We have beautiful summer weather now. What a joy! The children can play outside. They are all doing well, also the twins. Théo sits by himself now; Martha takes it more easy. We look forward to the time when we can load everyone into a railroad car and start back to our dear home! If only we were at that point. We can expect some more disappointments till then.

Good-bye for today. Keep healthy and well until we see you. We are in God's hand. He will do all things well.

Great-grandmother Hirschler
with whom Mother corresponded.

At La Jonchére in August 1940, preparing to return home to Schafbusch.

Return Trip to Schafbusch and the War Years
August 1940 to the Fall of 1944

Father: Since the beginning of the German offensive we hope for a change in the situation, which would allow us to return home. Then, in August 1940 we are asked to decide if we want to remain in France or

Our possessions are loaded on a two-wheeled cart for delivery to the train station at La Jonchére.

Possessions and family are loaded into our freight car. On the upper right is Uli and Alice.

return to the Alsace. Many Alsacians decide to stay in France, at least for the time being.

There is no future for us here. We prefer to return; nevertheless, not without concern. Again, we travel by freight train. This time my sister Lydia and her children are with us. My brother Oscar joins us in the first days of August after his discharge. He provides precious help in our travel preparations. The following details are taken from his diary:

On August 27 we receive the news that our return is scheduled for August 31. We build a number of standard wooden boxes for easy packing and good stacking in the railroad car. With our neighbor's two-wheeled cart and horse, we transport our baggage in two trips to the train in La Jonchère. On the steep, rocky path it is a perilous undertaking. Then we bid good-bye to Mr. and Mrs. Bonnaud, the retired couple who were always so helpful. On Saturday evening we leave La Jonchère-Saint-Maurice and travel through Guéret, Monlucon, and Givors as far as Lyon. On Sunday evening, when we reach Châlon-sur-Saône, we see the first German soldiers, who greet us with a good rice soup.

Our trip continues to Dijon, Vesoul, Belfort, and early Monday morning at 5:30 we stop in Mulhouse. A military band plays a welcome greeting and a mobile kitchen offers us milk coffee. At nine o'clock, again with band music, we start for Strasbourg. There, our wagon is unhooked from the train, while the others continue on to Keskastel and Saverne. We are stranded on the switching track. As I look around I notice a steaming

We make a train stop at Châlon-sur-Saône where we have hot soup.

locomotive. I ask the conductor where he is headed. His answer: "In the direction of Wissembourg!" He agrees to take us along. I don't know if the locomotive travels only for us, but at any rate, by 4 o'clock we arrive at Hunspach. That's as far as we can go; train service between Hunspach and Wissembourg has not yet been re-established. The station master from Haguenau had announced our coming in Wissembourg, so a bus as well as two trucks meet us and take us the last ten kilometers to Schafbusch.

At the Hunspach train station, we board a bus for the last six miles to Schafbusch.

Upon our return to Schafbusch, we found all our buildings were damaged. The house was made liveable again.

Mother: We are home again! We passed through times of testing and were often homesick; but, we also experienced the goodness and faithfulness of our Heavenly Father. We started out with fourteen children and return now with sixteen healthy children. It is September 2, 1940—a year and a day after we had left! We say with the psalmist: "Hitherto, the Lord has helped us." He will not abandon us!

Courage is what we need. Our house is still standing, but the roof has a big hole. All the windows are broken; the furniture has disappeared. The chaos outside is indescribable; everywhere debris of roof tiles, stones, parts of walls, and grenade holes. We find moldy mattresses in the trenches, and cooking pans in the manure pile. There are splintered trees and weeds the height of a man in the garden and in the fields. We fill up the holes, bury the rubbish, and salvage what can be used.

Father: All the buildings are damaged. My brother Willy arrived earlier and cleaned up the house of the worst rubbish; it is liveable. Geisberg, however, lies in total ruins, except for the house at the entrance. Lydia and her children live with us. Later Otto, with his family and my brothers, Oscar, Willy, and Walter, with his wife, come also. We manage somehow to house them all.

During the next years Willy will marry and move to Salmiak; Oscar will find work in other agricultural enterprises; Otto will be drafted into the army; and Walter will find employment with the area agricultural department (Kreisbauernschaft) and move to Wissembourg.

The laundry could be done at the pump in the center of the courtyard.

At first we are given food by the German government. A group of twelve men from the *Arbeitsdienst* (youth service) repairs the roof of our house at no cost. Oscar noted: "They needed 1,800 new roof tiles." We are given two cows, two horses, and even a tractor. Gradually most of the refugees return, especially the farmers. Everywhere plowing and sowing is being done. Much has changed and not always to our liking. The joy of being home again outweighs all that is unpleasant.

Dora: The French culture must be erased from our memories. The families are ordered under threat of the K.Z. (concentration camp) to destroy all literature in that language, and not to converse in French. All names like "Grandjean" or first names like "René" are to be legally replaced with German names. A strict censure makes all correspondence with our French friends, who had been so kind to us, impossible. On the other hand, we were to show enthusiastic gratitude to our liberators from the yoke of the French domination and for our return into the bosom of our "true" fatherland—Germany. Compared with the privileges gained, this intervention had ruined us—a small price to be paid! It was compulsory to have a picture of our benefactor and chief, "the Führer," in every home! There are pictures available at any price and taste: Adolph Hitler in uniform; romantic; in a park surrounded by deer; or as a friendly uncle playing with children.

Father: The South German Mennonites send help for the various families of our congregation who had suffered loss, for which we are grateful. The Geisberg chapel is also damaged and we meet each Sunday in our living room. In the euphoria of the first victorious war years, the plans for reconstruction by the German government are grandiose. There are plans to completely rebuild Schafbusch, including the main house. To begin with, the farm buildings are torn down. On the right, at the entrance of the courtyard, the first building is erected. It contains an apartment, a workshop, garages, and a granary. It was almost what I had asked for. My wish was for a longer, wider, and higher building. In those years a great number of buildings which could have been repaired were torn down. In the meantime, the German army experiences reverses and the government changes its tune. No other buildings will be erected.

The conditions to run the farm are no longer the same. Buildings, machines, manpower, and many other things are missing. It is impossible to get the results, as before the war, and the income is less. Ernest, and later Alfred, are called up, first for the *Arbeitsdienst* and later for military service (as very young soldiers). Toward the end of the war René also has to go, and in the very last days, Eric, too. For a time I am alone on the farm. Before that, René and Willy often have to miss school to help on the farm. Sometimes a group of prisoners of war is available—Russian officers; men from India, who come mostly in the evening; and sometimes they are German soldiers. We use them to thin out sugar beets to cut and tie flax or other jobs. Our children help a lot and students join them during vacation;

Some of the Schafbusch farm buildings were torn down to begin the German government's big plans for reconstruction. Only this first building was erected.

the latter are obligated to work on farms. Schoolchildren, with their teachers, are mobilized to pick potatoes. In 1944 a Polish family, which had been expelled from east Poland in 1939 by the Russians, comes to us—father, mother, grandmother, and three small children.

We plant wheat, oats, barley, rye, potatoes (less than before), some sugar beets, red beets, carrots, kohlrabi, flax, canola, poppies (for oil), mustard, turnips, clover, and even radishes. I divide the clover field into small lots and rent them to rabbit owners in Wissembourg. This initiative is greatly appreciated.

Dora: The need for textiles and shoes is not as great as in occupied France. Here the Alsace is not occupied, but annexed; nevertheless, there are strong restrictions and our parents do not deal on the black market. When it is warm enough, the schoolchildren go barefoot to the edge of town to save their shoes. We raise geese for feathers and we learn to comb sheep wool and spin. Socks and stockings are of poor quality and it takes five to six hours each week to do the mending. Mother patches shirts, jackets, and pants for her ten sons endlessly. She reinforces cuffs, collars, puts patches in elbows, knees, and seats of pants. She uses the bottom of worn out shirts to repair the top of another. In spite of all her efforts, she is unable to provide enough clothing for everyone. One day I find her shedding tears of helplessness sitting at her sewing machine—but not for long. As always, Mother quickly controls herself. For this reason, the younger brothers and sisters were never aware of these and other needs. They remember these days as happy times, free from worry.

And then, there are the questions of conscience. The Bible teaches us to submit to the authorities, for it is instituted by God. But which one? The one before 1939, or before 1914? The opinion of the people is divided. Shall we submit to the authority which is being defeated or the power that is coming? When do you change loyalty without becoming traitor or opportunist? We have friends in France; we have friends and relatives in Germany. Why must we always deny a part of ourselves? Couldn't we have friendly relationships on both sides and not be suspected as traitor? We are troubled in our faith. We feel attacked on our moral values, hard pressed for our sentiments. We are worried about our soldiers: Ernest in Russia and Alfred in Italy. Father, who according to Mennonite principles does not participate in politics, gradually becomes suspect. Added to this, as we learn later, a high official covets the farm for himself and does anything to make things nearly impossible for Father. The day comes when the *Kreisleiter* (District Governor) meets with Father in the field and threatens deportation to Poland for him and all his family. René witnessed the scene. It is during this time that our old aunt, Madeleine Hirschler, was secretly involved in giving shelter to political refugees. Only fifty years later did we learn of this.

Erica Hege Shirk tells the story after a visit in 1993 to Mother Odette, one of the refugees:

On one of his official visits the Lutheran Bishop of Hanover, Horst Hirschler, a distant relative, met Mother Odette, who is in charge of an Evangelical community of the Benedictine Order. Hearing his name reminded her of an elderly lady named Madeleine Hirschler. This lady, our great-aunt, hid her and another ten-year-old girl in the attic of our house during the summer of 1942 when her life was threatened because of her Jewish background. Through the efforts of the pastor at Steinseltz, Miss Bertsch, she came to Schafbusch.

Our Aunt Madeleine, at age seventy-eight, was the only contact person. She provided protection and safety—sometimes in her bedroom, most of the time in the attic under the eaves behind some blankets. A third teenage girl lived in the room with the aunt. Odette says: "The very being of the aunt radiated kindness and safety." She provided them with plenty of reading material and they read and read and read. There was nothing else to do.

The noises of daily life in the house, especially lots of happy laughter, and the coming and going from morning to evening, made them feel secure.

Unknown to the Hege children, Aunt Madeleine Hirschler secretly hid some political refugees in her room at Schafbusch in 1942.

At the same time, the fear of being discovered was always with them, like when they had to go to the toilet. Twice they had to vacate because there was the possibility the house would be searched. The first time the ambulance from Wissembourg came and took them for a drive until it was safe to return. The second time Miss Bertsch came to the farm with a group of children and when they left, the two girls were in the group. Odette is sure there were hundreds of such people passing through the area, and others, besides the three that we know of, were hiding at Schafbusch. Our parents never talked about it, not even in later years. Surely they were informed; the aunt could hardly feed three extra people without their knowledge.

Feelings of peace, joy, and security surface as Odette remembers this summer in her life. With gratefulness she says, "I would not be here today if it had not been for your Aunt Madeleine."

The end of the war is not far away. The Americans are coming closer—the "good" chasing the "bad." The fighting will have to pass through our region and we are dreading what is coming. I ask myself, "Is it really necessary for fighter bombers to harass the civilian population, and to shoot at women and children in the streets and fields?"

Our Flight to Willenbach
December 1944 to May 1945

Father: In the fall of 1944, the front comes closer; the sounds of canon fire become more and more noticeable. German soldiers occupy the farm, setting up artillery around the buildings and in the fields. We transform our cellar into a bomb shelter—not very adequately, for we are determined to stay here, come what may. Since the beginning of December 1944, on orders of the Civil Defense office at Karlsruhe, René is stationed in Wissembourg with our two horses. For some time the front is stalled in the Haguenau Forest. For this reason the German administration has time to take measures which they could not take in other parts of the Alsace. All men between ages sixteen and sixty-six are called up by the Civil Defense under threat of death and must regroup on the east side of the Rhine. This involves Eric and myself. As an alternative each man can choose to take his family with him into Germany. If he does, he is exempt from the military.

Dora: I share a few excerpts which follow from my sister Irène's diary. She was a math student and returned home because of the circumstances. She did her work with zeal and devotion, which characterized her.

Thursday, November 23, 1944: *The front comes closer. The first soldiers stop and ask for food and want to dry their clothes.*

Saturday, November 25: *Twenty-five soldiers are stationed on the farm. There is intense activity in the skies.*

Tuesday, November 28: *Yeast is no longer available for bread baking, but someone gives us a recipe to make more yeast, using ten grams of yeast and adding water, sugar, flour, and potatoes. It works quite well.*

Friday, December 1: *Our noon meal is potato soup, cream of wheat (with 5 lbs. of cream of wheat and 10 liters of milk), served with 4 liters of wine sauce.*

Saturday, December 2: *Our Polish worker receives orders to report to Wissembourg with his family.*

Monday, December 4: *Our two horses are confiscated. René is ordered to take them to Wissembourg.*

Tuesday, December 5: *We bake bread with 92 lbs. of flour, using the new yeast. The bread is excellent.*

Thursday, December 7: *We receive orders to dig trenches along the road. But there is continuous rain; the ground is so wet and heavy that we give up after 20 minutes. Our group is made up of Father, Offerle, our old farmhand, Eric, Erica, Sonja, our household help, and myself.*

Friday, December 8: *We try again and dig for half an hour.*

Saturday, December 9: *I was digging all morning and until two in the afternoon; then I am called home; all the men between ages 16 and 66 are called up. Eric and Offerle are called and have to leave. Father is given a week deferment.*

Sunday, December 10: *We learn the men in the Civilian Defense are stationed near Heilbronn. In the afternoon I dig from 1 to 3 o'clock.*

Monday, December 11: *In the afternoon I dig until 3:30, then we are excused because of the rain. Artillery shooting gets louder.*

Tuesday, December 12: *Father's deferment is annulled; we must leave today.*

Father: Suddenly, a conviction, I believe God inspired, takes hold of me. We must leave and go to Willenbach. My relative, Walter Landes, has been urging us repeatedly to come to their farm for safety. He lives on the 160 ha (400 acre) property of Willenbach near Heilbronn, about 130 km (80 miles) distance. Some of the soldiers also encourage us to leave. That is why on December 12 we again pack our suitcases. We load two wagons with our belongings and again forget to take along many important things.

Mother: A military truck is ready to take us to the train station. We are: Lydia with six children; Dina and her five sons; myself with ten of our children; a household help; and our eighty-year-old Aunt Madeleine Hirschler. Each carries a backpack and a blanket. Before we leave the house, we gather for a last time in the dining room and Father prays for protection of Almighty God for his family. It is 6 o'clock in the evening and it is dark. We reach the last train which leaves Wissembourg before the arrival of the Americans. During the day the train station was bombed; the train windows are broken and the wet seats are covered with pieces of glass. We are not allowed to turn lights on until all windows are covered with blankets. We make ourselves comfortable as best as we can. The train travels all night and arrives in Heidelberg in the early morning hours. We are tired and worn out from this uncomfortable night, except for twelve-year-old Uli. He promptly pulls out a thermometer and chart from his backpack; this took the place of his pajamas and toothbrush (these stayed at home instead). He proceeds to record the temperature for the weather station in Colmar, as he did every day at home. We spend the day in Heidelberg at a center for refugees. Our next train leaves at dusk. Finally, we are on our way to Heilbronn. There are a few other passengers. Now someone starts a song. Christmas is ten days away. We sing the beautiful Christmas carols, one after another, as we have done many times at home. Gradually the weight of our plight is lightened and our hearts are encouraged.

Dora: The atmosphere on the train was tense; at any time we could expect an air attack. Of course, it was Mother who began to sing and the children joined in. I, for my part, could not sing.

Mother: Around midnight we stop in Bad Friedrichshall-Jagstfeld. The train station of Heilbronn, as well as the town, had recently been destroyed by an air attack. It is too late to call Willenbach. We spend the night in an overcrowded waiting room. It is cold; the children cry from hunger and cold. Aunt Lydia shares dried bread she had brought along. Early the next morning they come from Willenbach with a tractor and wagon, and a horse-drawn carriage to pick us up. (Gasoline is scarce and horse-drawn carriages are used again. There are plenty of these on the property, from the simple open buggy to the covered coach.) We are warmly welcomed, given food, and can warm ourselves. The house is already full of refugees from Heilbronn and other places. But in spite of it, they make room for our family and for Aunt Madeleine. Dina and her children find refuge with a Schmutz family at the Sulzhof/Möckmühl; Lydia and her children are taken in by the Hege family in Markt/Augsburg.

Father: With Willy and Fritz, I take to the road with one of the wagons pulled by two oxen. We have no lights and it is dark and raining. Since we must travel at the pace of the animals, short distances only, we plan to "Mennonite our way" by going from one Mennonite farm to another. Our first stop is Deutschhof, near Bergzabern, with my sister Frieda. Here our second wagon waits for us; it had been picked up earlier by a nephew and a prisoner of war. We continue on to the Hege family in Landau, and then cross the Rhine at Speyer.

At the Kohlhof near Schifferstadt we borrow a pair of horses. Each night we sleep at a different farm: in Duren near Wieslach; with the Schmutz family in Bockschaft; at Phillip Fellmanns' in Rappenau; and with others. Finally, on December 24 we arrive at Oscar Fellmanns' in Wimpfen where we leave our oxen. In the meantime, Willenbach sends a tractor to bring us to our destination. Tired, but in good health and unharmed, we celebrate Christmas together with our family. Later we learn that our house burned down on December 13, the night after we left.

Dora: Fritz, who was then age thirteen, later wrote about this trip from Schafbusch to Willenbach with the wagon and oxen.

The story, as Fritz tells it:

On Tuesday, December 12, we are suddenly told we must leave. We begin packing right away. We pack mostly clothing. At first we were told we could use a Bulldog tractor. At noon Willy, age fifteen, applied for the one at the farmers cooperative. Since only one of the Bulldog tractors was left, they didn't want to give it to him. So, it was decided to use the oxen, Peter and Felix, to pull the wagon with our baggage. In the evening, after the others had left by car for the train station, we started on our way. It was about 7:30 in the evening and we arrived at Deutschhof around 11:30. The next day Willy and I returned to Steinseltz on bicycles to get legal papers for leaving. We had dinner at the mayor's house. He had reinforced his cellar with extra supports and planned to remain, come what may. Then we went up the hill to Schafbusch. What we saw was discouraging. The soldiers had already taken many things. Several pigs had been butchered. They had loaded all the apples into their cars. The next day we went on to Landau. We stayed there until Sunday. During that time Father wanted to make contact with the rest of the family at Willenbach. When he came back he told us that we would need to leave right away that evening for Speyer. So we drove to Speyer during the night. All of a sudden two tanks that were tied together came by. The second one caught the bicycles on the back of our wagon and twisted the front wheels.

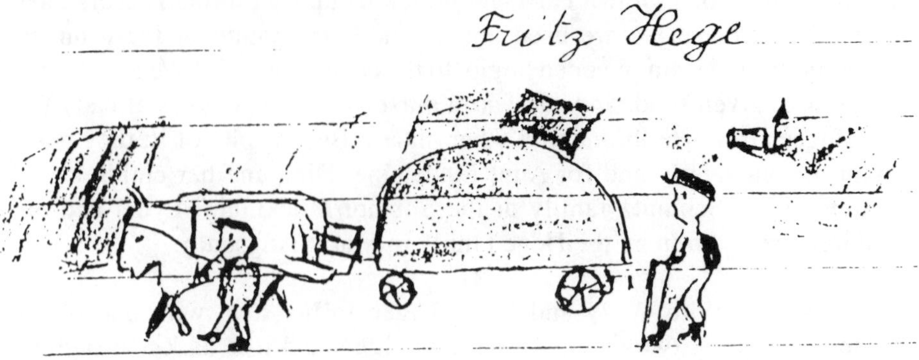

We arrived in Speyer the next morning at 6 o'clock. There we created quite a sensation. When we continued at noon one of the oxen started to bleed on one foot. Father left us at the Rhine bridge. We stopped in the next village. Willy went to the mayor's office and asked for a place to spend the night. In the meantime, I waited at the market place. Suddenly, Peter knocked a small boy down. A large crowd gathered around us. Each one had a suggestion of what I should have done. We stayed for two nights in their accommodations. The people took fairly good care of us. On the second day we had the oxen shod and one bicycle repaired. Then we continued on our way. Everywhere we were asked where we were coming from and where we were going. The next night we stayed in Rauenberg. Then we went to Duren. There we also stayed one day. Then Father came back to us. Now we traveled together until Bockschaft. Father went ahead of us with the horses. Before Rappenau a team of horses from Willenbach met us. These were exchanged for the oxen. We led the oxen as far as Wimpfen and put them there in a barn. We had to walk the whole day, otherwise the oxen would not have moved. On December 24, at 8 in the evening, we arrived at Willenbach.

-Fritz Hege

Dora: Gradually life in Willenbach finds a rhythm. We are a community of about 100 persons, including the Landes family and personnel.

The Landis family home at Willenbach when the Heges arrive.

All ages and social standings are represented—city dwellers and farmers, brought together through the same trials: loss or absence of dear family members and loss of home and belongings. Uncle Walter and Aunt Helene (who later became Alfred's and Willy's parents-in-law) do their best to care for our well being and try to smooth out the corners. Modest or influential, related, befriended, or just acquainted, all are treated with equal courtesy.

Each one tries to make himself useful. We start a kindergarten, a first, and second grade class. Because of the increasing air attacks of the Americans, we are tied to the house more and more. We are awakened at night by the eerie whining of English and American bombers which fly over us by the hundreds to destroy the cities nearby and in the distance,

The Landis family home at Willenbach after the war came through in April 1945.

killing women and children by the thousands. We see men, party members, gradually losing all haughtiness. One of the uniforms was discretely buried in the ground. The cellar is fixed up for an eventual longer stay. The front line comes near and remains stationary near Willenbach. On April 2, an SS-battalion sets up a command post in the immense vaulted cellar of the "chateau." We also seek shelter there. At one end where a stairway leads into the house are the Landes family and their employees and the refugees. The children are confined to the big storage shelves for apples. The adults sit on straw and piles of potatoes. A bed is brought in for our seriously-ill father. At the other end of the cellar we find the twenty-five farm laborers, mainly deported Poles and Ukrainians, some with family. In all, we were about 110 persons. The part in the middle, near the outside steps, is reserved for the military. The radio operators put up their installations; a dozen SS-soldiers come and go; wounded soldiers are given first aid and leave again.

We are really in very crowded quarters. One night I get awake and see, a few yards away, a circle of officers talking to each other in the light of a lantern. I hear them discussing new weapons which will soon be available and give a final victory! It is the 6th or 7th of April 1945. For several days Willenbach is the center of the fighting. The buildings burn down, one after another. The house, which is hit too, holds up the longest. The animals have been untied and roam the fields. In moments of quiet the men venture out to milk the cows and to put an end to wounded animals. We lack neither milk nor meat, and get a warm meal every day. The cook and her helpers accomplish miracles on the small makeshift stove in the cellar. Often, the "staff" also uses the regular stove in the kitchen which then causes renewed shooting because of the visible smoke coming from the chimney. The smoke from the stove in the cellar could not be noticed by the search planes overhead. When the heavy artillery is fired and fear begins to take hold of us, Uncle Walter starts to sing one of the many hymns of faith. He knows all the verses by memory and we sing until fear is replaced with peace and trust. On Sunday, after Easter, as we are eating breakfast, we again hear heavy shooting. A soldier comes running in with the news that the house is in flames. There is no more water available to put out the fire; we must leave the house.

The captain of the SS unit allows us to use a truck, although it is strictly forbidden to help the civilian population because of the scarcity of gas. We take a few of our belongings. As we step out into the bright daylight, we squint. Only burned out walls are left from the farm buildings. The cattle roam in the wheat fields and the flames crackle behind us. Fiery tiles are falling from the roof. Watch out! We climb on the truck. Father is carried on a stretcher; he is so weak that he passes out as soon as he tries to get up. We drive to the Lautenbach farm a few miles distant. It is spring and the air is mild with radiant sunshine. We can't grasp what we see. Even branches hard hit by grenades have young leaves of wonderful delicate green. An airplane circles overhead. Suddenly, two sparkling objects in the sunshine! Bombs fall and explode not far from the bridge we are crossing. After 4 km (3 miles) we reach Lautenbach, an even larger farm property managed by two brothers of Uncle Walter, Christian and Ernst Landes.

Normally about 100 persons live here, but with the refugees, there are many more. We find normal, or almost normal, Sunday activities. It is quiet, people are dressed in Sunday clothes, and the surroundings are peaceful. Yet, people avoid spending time outside, for the enemy planes are everywhere. The real war, however, seems far away. Just to be safe, they direct us to stay in the cellar. Organizational rules need to be worked out.

House Rules At Lautenbach During the Occupation

1. Because of the special circumstances of the war, Lautenbach is giving shelter to an unusual number of persons. For this reason there has to be a set of regulations to make sure that everyone on the farm is safely taken care of.

2. The farm is divided into the following sub-groups:

a) main house:	
living quarters:	= Herr Renkert
cellar:	= Herr v. d. Smissen
b) upper house:	= Herr Krieger
c) lower house:	= Herr Ernest Landes
d) gardener's house:	= Frau Schneider
e) upper potato cellar:	= Tante Emma (Schafbusch)
f) lower potato cellar:	= Herr Seitz
g) other single houses and apartments:	= heads of each household

The persons named are appointed the person in charge of each group.

3. The person in charge is responsible for the care of all the people in his group and brings any request to Mr. Christian Landes.

4. All occupants at the farm must take shelter when airplanes approach and may under no circumstances move around.

Lautenbach, the farm of Christian and Ernst Landes. We are welcomed and cared for here too.

5. The person in charge must appoint one person from the group who is responsible to see that the children take immediate cover as soon as airplanes approach.

6. All ammunition found must be handed over at the upper house. Children shall in no way play with it.

7. Mealtimes:

Breakfast:	6:30 a.m. to 8:30 a.m.	
Lunch:	11 a.m.	
Evening meal:	cellar 5:30 p.m.	main house 6 p.m.

8. All use of paper, also toilet paper, is to be used sparingly, since the supply is low.

9. It is not permitted to leave the farm or the park, since the entrance of the park toward Oedheim is seen by the enemy. Any movement of people can provoke artillery fire.

April 1945

We are welcomed and cared for with the same kindness and generosity as in Willenbach. A few days later, on April 12, 1945, the Germans withdraw. The war for us is over; the bad days, however, not yet. Now anarchy takes over; the former prisoners and those deported by force are the masters. They plunder, steal, feast, and drink. Here and there they torture or kill their former masters to get even for ill treatment. Nothing happens in Lautenbach, but we try to be careful. Gradually the American administration takes control. They set up a curfew.

It is during this time that our brother, Uli, slips into a shed where he discovers some weapons left by the soldiers. It is strictly forbidden to touch them, but he wants to know how they function. He fingers a bazooka that has the top unscrewed, and it explodes. Our brother is badly burned on the chest and face, and poisoned by the gasses he inhales. He is taken to the hospital in Neckarsulm, which is overcrowded with the sick and wounded. They have neither running water nor electricity, and no receptionist. They are short on personnel and have only one doctor. Curfew is lifted for only two hours, morning and afternoon. It takes just about that much time to walk from Lautenbach to Neckarsulm and back. Therefore, Eric and I have little time when we visit him two days later. It would not have been wise to take a bicycle because of the many plunderers roaming the land who could not be trusted. Uli doesn't look good, he is tortured by thirst, and holds tightly to a water bottle which he is unwilling to let go. We don't have the experience to know just how serious his condition is. He will die six hours later, all alone. The doctor, a woman whom I find in the office, is tired from overwork. She assures me Uli is no longer in danger. The next day it is Erica and Willy's turn to visit him. They find the bed empty. No one can tell them where he is and finally they discover him in a bathroom, naked and stretched out on the floor. He is dead. That was on April 18. The body is brought to Lautenbach; there is no coffin available. The carpenter on the property fashions a box-like coffin. To bury him in the cemetery in the village of Oedheim nearby, we must have a special permission to be allowed on the road. We receive it for the use of a tractor and trailer. Father is still too weak and is not able to come along. Mother, until now always so brave, gets sick, too. She will never completely get over the loss of this son. Whenever she is reminded of him, her eyes fill with tears.

End Of War And Rebuilding

May 1945 to 1954

The war is over; life continues. Ten days after the funeral there is a happy event. On April 30, Ernest returns in good health. On May 2, he and Willy set out on bicycles to investigate Schafbusch. This prospect gives new strength to our parents. We check the cellar in Willenbach to see what remains of our baggage. It suffered little damage from the fire and looting. Our friends supply us with provisions, dishes, cooking pots, etc. On May 17, we take our leave from the Landes family, our hearts filled with gratitude for all they had done for us. In the future a border will separate us from these relatives; the Alsace has become French again. However, we look forward to seeing our French friends once again.

With a trailer load of suitcases, sacks, and boxes, we set out for the train station in Heilbronn, expecting to be home by evening. We are: Father, Mother, Dora, Irène, Eric, Erica, Fritz, Alice, Oscar, Hans, Louise, Martha, Théo, and Aunt Madeleine. The latter sits on a stretcher which we carry. The families of Aunt Dina and Aunt Lydia will come later.

We have hardly begun to unload our baggage when two American soldiers come up and forbid us to take anything but hand baggage! (Strict measures had just been issued to control plundering.) All our pleadings and explanation go unheeded; almost everything must be left behind. When the watchmen don't seem to be looking, we, nevertheless, take seven sacks; each contains a feather bed. Father decides that Fritz should stay in Lautenbach, hoping that a few days later he could bring the baggage. This was not to happen; Fritz joins us on July 16. We receive the baggage only two years later and this, thanks to the efforts of MCC (Mennonite Central Committee).

The train gets moving. We are on our way home! However, when we arrive at the French zone, we are integrated into the flow of those deported, such as former prisoners of war and French forced laborers. We must pass through various repatriation camps. We are held up in Mannheim for a few days and in Speyer, and later summoned to Strasbourg within a few weeks after we arrived home at Schafbusch. We pass through several health controls and repeated questionings. We are checked by doctors and disin-

The house at Schafbusch when the Heges return in 1945.

fected with DDT. To accomplish this we are dusted with much white powder with the help of huge syringes. The steps in front of the building look like a flour mill. They are covered with white dust. We are then questioned individually by suspicious military personnel about the reasons for our stay in Germany. Are we victims or offenders? Deportees? Or, traitors and war criminals? Our statements are questioned and we barely escape being sent to a French concentration camp, from the oldest to the youngest. Fortunately, Father has no enemies and they finally believe us. Our large family is constantly in conflict with the regulations that are meant for single persons. To the authorities we are a source of embarrassment, irritation, and continual headache.

Finally, on May 24, it is decided to take us directly to Schafbusch. A robust lady sergeant commands us to climb into a van, together with our seven sacks of bedding. Does she consider us to be mental cases and all of us scoundrels? How roughly she treats us! I am indignant! Yes, we are guilty; that is, guilty of existing!

And, finally we arrive at home, much discouraged, humiliated, and tired. Our hearts are bleeding that Uli is no longer with us. We know nothing of Alfred and René. We have practically nothing to sustain us. At Schafbusch there is no food, no stove, no dishes, no change of clothes, nothing to sit on, nothing for sleeping except our seven feather beds, neither lights nor telephone, no means of transportation, no tools, nor any animals. But we are happy to find Ernest and Willy there.

What used to be our home are burned out walls. We are now fifteen persons. We try to make ourselves at home in the small apartment at one end of the long building at the right of the entrance. It is badly damaged, but can be repaired. The farm, as a whole, is partially destroyed and plundered of everything. They had even begun to take the tiles off the roof and dig up plants from the garden. Rumors had spread that the Hege family was not coming back. But we must give credit to the people from the village; all our farm machinery was returned, sometimes secretly.

Mother: What a pitiful sight! The pump in the middle of the courtyard is still standing, our good old pump, and there is fresh, clear water. What a gift! The neighbor lady appears with a pot of good soup. We take turns eating; we don't even have enough plates and spoons. The brother-in-law, Ehrismann, brings straw in place of mattresses. The smallest of our children can find a place at Geisberg for awhile. The families of Geisberg also followed our example in December and fled to German Mennonites for a time. However, their farms had less damage and they had returned earlier.

And the new life begins. Gradually help comes from all sides, deeply moving us. Farmers come, some with bread, potatoes, flour, butter, a ham; others with dishes, beds, clothing, and even a sewing machine.

Life begins in the small apartment at the end of the long building. Mother and the children take the baked goods to the still useable brick oven in the old house.

A 1961 aerial view of Schafbusch located on the left side of the highway.

A woman gives us a hen with ten chicks. We find potatoes in the silo and some dishes in the rubble. Then the Mennonites from the Haut-Rhin organize help for our congregation. And later packages from our brothers and sisters in America start arriving. A group of reconstruction workers, American Mennonite volunteers, come to Wissembourg to help with rebuilding. René returns on June 1 by the way of Switzerland with clean-shaven head. Alfred became an American prisoner of war in Italy. He is the last to come home on July 13; he is thin but still in good health. This fills our hearts with gratitude.

Father: The situation is worse than in 1940. Not only do we have a lot of damage, but the whole area is impoverished and devastated. Together we get to work. The small apartment, which we fix up as best as we can, is very confining. Later, we are assigned a barrack. Sometime later I am able to buy two more barracks.

Mother: Everything we do takes much time. The essentials are missing on all sides and there are endless difficulties. The following winter is very hard. Bedrooms are damp and ice cold; several of our children become seriously ill. In spite of it, our situation gradually improves. We are very grateful that we could return and live here in peace. We find strength again. We are filled with new courage and can say with the psalmist, "The Lord has done great things for us whereof we are glad." (Psalm 126:3)

Father: The fields, too, have suffered from the war. We had to painstakingly fill about 120 shell craters before we were able to harvest the 1.5 ha (4 acres) of wheat which we had planted the previous fall. The government assigned us two horses and several cows. Thanks to the Marshal Plan we are able to buy a Farmall tractor for about 1,000frs. That is the cost of a horse. The sale of the mirabelles which we picked that summer amounted to about that much. I am able to take out a loan from the Farmers' Credit Union. We find our Bulldog tractor in a neighboring village and get it running. Fertilizer and fuel are scarce, as well as many other necessary things. Little by little, the farm operation gets going again and the buildings are temporarily repaired. We are able to salvage the kitchen range and the ceramic tile stove from the rubble of the old house.

The first three Massey-Harris combines are delivered in the Alsace in 1948. Our American volunteers, living in Wissembourg, encourage me to buy one. The following year I am able to obtain a hay and straw baler to go with it. Each is equipped with its own engine and has to be pulled with the tractor. The grain is bagged in the field. In this way the harvest is much easier. It is a sensation for the farmers of the area! The fields begin to produce good harvests; however, the reconstruction of our house makes no progress. We make plans, then must change them again; our suggestions are only partially accepted. By the end of 1952 there is finally a green light. Work begins in the spring of 1953, and it is finished by the end of 1954. The house has just been finished when lightning strikes and the roof burns off. With a temporary roof, we move in anyhow. By the end of October the roof is repaired. Now, after ten years, we finally have enough room. After several years we begin to grow peas for the canning factory in Wissembourg, and the "Bintge" variety of potatoes sells well. We enlarge our herd of cattle and sell milk to the dairy in Riedseltz. Later we grow corn instead of peas and potatoes. Otto leaves with his family and settles at the Freihof in Neufgrange near Saarguemines.

In the meantime though, our family is beginning to scatter. Several of our children are married. Erica marries one of the Mennonite volunteers and moves to Pennsylvania in the United States of America. Just like we have always said, "Our Erica goes to America." From Irène's diary we have this record of the wedding reception on the next page.

Wedding Reception
on
August 21, 1948
For
Erica and Frank

Number of invited guests estimated between eighty to a hundred.

Menu
Patty shells (Bouchée à la reine)
Cold ham and mixed salads with mayonnaise
with homemade rolls
Raspberry ice cream and cake
Coffee and cookies

Refreshments after the ceremony
Gugelhopf
Streussel cake
Braided loaves
Coffee and milk

Preparations: All the cookies were baked earlier: meringue, vanilla pretzel, cut-out cookies, anise cookies, spritz cookies, and anise slices.

Thursday, August 19: We bake the cakes. We have 20 cake pans which we put in the large bake oven after the bread is done. (We had baked bread using 66 lbs. flour.) 114 eggs were beaten by hand with about 10 lbs. sugar and mixed with 7 1/2 lbs. flour and 5 lemons. Half the cakes are filled with vanilla cream filling and the other half with chocolate cream filling, covered with lemon or chocolate icing.

Friday, August 20: The day to make yeast dough; in the big trough it is kneaded by hand and baked in the brick oven used for bread. We use 77 lbs. flour, 70 eggs, 13 lbs. sugar, 16 qts. milk, 2 lbs. yeast, raisins. This makes 20 streusel cakes, 16 *gugelhopf* and braided breads.

Saturday, August 21: Bake rolls early in the morning with 20 lbs. flour, 3 qts. milk, 1 1/4 lbs. butter, salt.

Patty shells: Come from the bakery; we give the baker the necessary ingredients (we are limited with food stamps): 7 lbs. flour, 8 eggs, 2 1/2 lbs. butter.

The filling: From the farm: 4 chickens, 3 cans ground meat
From the butcher: 11 lbs. veal, 2 lbs. bacon
From the grocery store: 2 cans mushrooms

Cold ham: 3 hams from the farm

Salads: 55 lbs. tomatoes (50 lbs. were bought), 25 lbs. beans, 33 lbs. cauliflower, 7 lbs. carrots, onions and parsley from the garden, 2 qts. vinegar and oil

Ice Cream: 18 qts. milk, 3 qts. canned raspberries, 12 eggs from the farm, condensed milk, and sugar. It was made by Fanny Gingerich with the help of the Mennonite volunteers and their ice cream freezer.

Summary of ingredients

130 lbs. flour (a gift from MCC of America)
42 lbs. sugar (also from MCC)
2 1/2 lbs. powdered sugar
28 1/2 lbs. butter (bought wholesale)
4 1/4 lbs. lard and oil
383 eggs
59 qts. milk
2 3/4 lbs. yeast
10 lemons
1 lb. chocolate
1/2 lb. cornstarch
2 lbs. coffee

In 1967, on Grandmother Hege's 70th birthday surrounded by the Hege children and their families.

Philipp and Emma Hege with their children in 1967, from the left in front: Erica, Dora, parents, Irène, and Alice. Middle row: Oscar, Théo, Eric, Louise, Martha, Alfred, and Hans. Back row: Willy, Fritz, Ernest, and René.

The Schafbusch residence was reconstructed in 1954. The farm property continues to be owned and operated by the Hege family.

Closing Words

In 1958 it seemed to me it was the right time to rent the farm to René, the only farmer among my sons. Several of his brothers already owned their businesses. In 1966 I turned the farm over to René on favorable terms. Cattle raising and milk production proved to be very unprofitable. In 1963 we sell most of our cattle, and René specializes in chickens; first producing and selling eggs, later raising pullets. He builds a large chicken house in which he raises about 50,000 chicks and sells them as laying hens to egg-producing farmers. At the same time, he intensifies corn production and installs a corn dryer. In 1976 one-half of the fields produce corn; on the remaining fields, 2/3 are in wheat and 1/3 in canola.

We have known many tests and hardships, but also much joy and satisfaction. Our way of life and methods of farming have radically changed. Our God has remained faithful and has blessed us richly. He heard the prayers of my father, who was missing in Russia, concerning his family and property. The future, also, is in His hands.

Philipp and Emma Hege taken on her 80th birthday.

As we think of our many grandchildren we pray God daily to keep them from the evil one and to lead them to salvation on the narrow way. May His blessing continue to rest on our descendants.

Philipp Hege, 1976-1979